MW00682506

States

School Specialty Publishing

Columbus, Ohio

Send all inquiries to:
School Specialty Publishing
8720 Orion Place
Columbus, OH 43240-2111

ISBN 0-7696-5503-3

2 3 4 5 6 7 8 9 10 POH 09 08

Table of Contents

Hawaii

Aloha! That expression means "love" in Hawaiian, and it is used to say "hello" and "goodbye." The state of Hawaii is a group of islands located in the middle of the north Pacific Ocean. Many of the islands are so small that no one lives on them permanently.

The Hawaiian Islands were first settled by Polynesian people who traveled there from other Pacific islands. Before becoming a state, the islands had several kinds of governments. For over a hundred years, Polynesian monarchs ruled. Today, you can visit some of the palaces where they once lived. The last monarch, Queen Liliuokalani, was the author of the favorite Hawaiian song, "Aloha Oe," or "Farewell to Thee." In 1893, Hawaii became a republic with elected leaders. It was made a United States territory in 1900. In 1959, Hawaii became the fiftieth state.

Hawaii produces tropical crops, especially pineapples, sugar, and coffee. However, its biggest industry is tourism. People come for the warm air, the clean beaches, the beautiful landscape, and the good shopping. Like the visitors, Hawaii's people come from all over the world. No ethnic group is in the majority there.

The Hawaiian island with the biggest population is Oahu, where the capital, Honolulu, is located. Near Honolulu is Pearl Harbor. A Japanese attack on the U.S. naval base there thrust the United States into World War II.

The island of Hawaii is often called the Big Island because it is the largest in the state. There, at Hawaii Volcanoes National Park, you may be able to see active volcanoes spewing lava, superhot liquid rock from deep underground. In fact, all the state's islands were formed by cooled lava that turned into land. Popular tourist attractions on the island of Kauai include Mount Waialeale, which has the most rainy days on earth, and Waimea Canyon.

Read the clues about Hawaii.
Then complete the puzzle using the word list on the next page.

★ *Across* ★

4. Hawaii was one just before it became a state.
5. Capital of Hawaii
7. Name of the harbor attacked by Japan that caused the United States to enter World War II
9. The most populated island in the state of Hawaii
10. Hawaiian greeting
11. Hawaii lies in the middle of the north Pacific _____.

12. Nickname for the island of Hawaii—the _____ Island

★ *Down* ★

1. Name of Hawaii's last queen
2. Hawaii is famous for this fruit.
3. Hawaii's largest industry
4. The ones on Mauna Kea are the largest in the world.
6. Volcanic material that originally formed the islands
8. Hawaiian royalty lived in these.

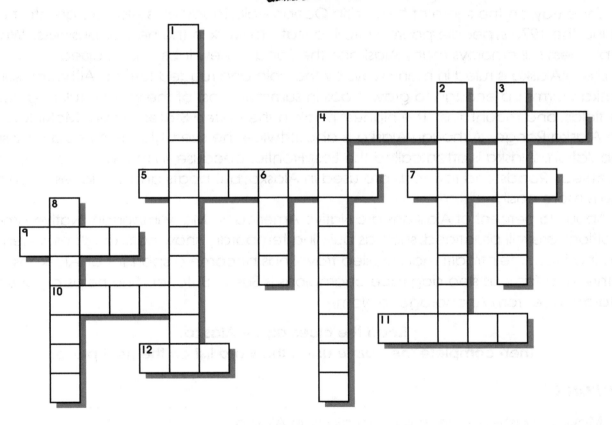

Word List

ALOHA	LILIUOKALANI	PALACES	TELESCOPES
BIG	OAHU	PEARL	TERRITORY
HONOLULU	OCEAN	PINEAPPLE	TOURISM
LAVA			

Alaska

Alaska lies at the northwest tip of North America. It is separated from the main body of the United States by part of Canada. The state is so far north that much of it is continually covered with snow and ice. Yet Alaska is an enormously valuable state.

In the mid-1800's, Russia and the United States both wanted Alaska because of its position as a gateway between Asia and America—and because of its valuable fur trade. After the United States bought Alaska from Russia, gold was discovered. This discovery led to a gold rush and the founding of Juneau, which is now Alaska's capital. Alaska became a state just before Hawaii, in 1959. Nine years later, the most valuable resource of all was found at Prudhoe Bay, on the shore of the Arctic Ocean—oil. Today, oil is Alaska's greatest export. During the 1970's, people poured into the state to work in the new oil business. While the oil business still employs many Alaskans, the flood of new jobs has stopped.

Life in Alaska is ruled in many ways by the cold and rugged terrain. Although southern Alaska warms up enough to grow crops in summer, most of the state is full of glaciers, ice fields, and mountains. The highest peak in the United States, Mount McKinley, is in the Alaska Range. Although Alaska is about twice the size of Texas, it has a very small population. Alaska is often called the Last Frontier because so much of the land remains unsettled. Roads and railroads are used in Alaska, but boats and airplanes often reach towns more easily.

About 15 percent of Alaskans are Native Americans. Many important Native American traditions are still practiced, such as building temporary snow huts, or igloos, when on hunting trips. Their traditional dogsled travel has become a sport for all Alaskans. One of the most famous sled dog race champions is Susan Butcher. She helps organize the Iditarod race from Anchorage to Nome.

Read the clues about Alaska.
Then complete the puzzle using the word list on the next page.

★ Across ★

2. Moving masses of ice; there are many in Alaska
3. Name of Alaska's most famous sled dog race
6. Temporary round hut made of snow blocks
8. Country from which the United States bought Alaska
10. Alaska is about twice as big as this state.
11. Last name of a sled dog race champion
12. Country that lies between Alaska and the lower forty-eight states

★ Down ★

1. Name of the bay where oil was first discovered in Alaska
2. Mineral resource that caused a rush to Alaska
4. Form of transportation first used by Native Americans in Alaska and northern Canada
5. Percentage of Alaskans who are Native Americans
7. Alaska's most valuable export
8. Capital of Alaska

Alaska's flag shows the Big Dipper pointing to the North Star.

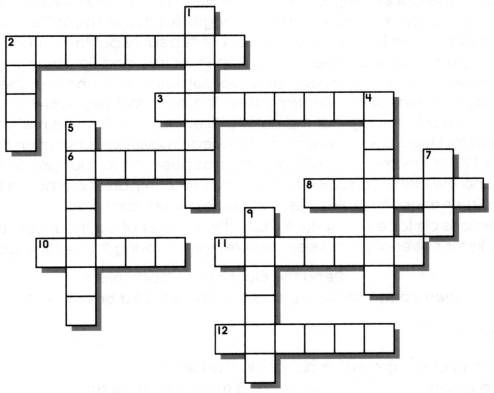

Word List

BUTCHER	GLACIERS	IGLOO	PRUDHOE
CANADA	GOLD	JUNEAU	RUSSIA
DOGSLED	IDITAROD	OIL	TEXAS
FIFTEEN			

California

California, here I come! That's what many people have said since 1848. Beginning with the discovery of gold in that year, newcomers from all over the United States and the world have made the Golden State their home. Today, California has the largest population of all the states in the union. Over 25 percent of Californians are Hispanic, and nearly 10 percent are Asian. California has acted as a gateway to the United States for these people or their ancestors. It is located northwest of Mexico and the rest of Spanish-speaking Central and South America, and east of Asia, which is across the Pacific Ocean.

You can find almost every kind of landscape in California. The state's long coast on the Pacific Ocean includes foggy redwood groves in the north and expansive, sunny beaches in the south. The Coast Ranges and the tall Sierra Nevada run through the state from north to south. Between these mountain ranges lies the warm, fertile Central Valley.

People may come to California because of its beauty but they often stay because of the state's great resources. The cities of San Francisco and Sacramento, now the state capital, grew during the gold rush. However, settlers soon found that the state's real treasure lay in the soil of the Central Valley. The fruits and vegetables that grow there year-round are sold throughout the nation. The huge Los Angeles metropolitan area is best known for Hollywood, where many American movies and television shows are made. Since the 1970's, another part of California has been in the spotlight: Silicon Valley, the area around the city of San Jose. Many computer companies are based there and have brought big changes to businesses and homes worldwide.

Californians do face one serious worry: the danger of earthquakes. But the threat of earthquakes is not enough to keep people from enjoying the unique California lifestyle.

Read the clues about California.
Then complete the puzzle using the word list on the next page.

★ Across ★

2. A shaking of the ground; a danger in California
5. Name of ranges of California hills and mountains near the sea
7. Movie capital of the United States
8. California has more of these than any other state.
11. Name of the valley where most fruits and vegetables grow in California
12. One of California's most valuable natural resources today

★ Down ★

1. Country bordering California to the southeast
3. Tree that grows along the foggy northern California coast
4. Name given to the valley where many computer makers work
6. California's tallest mountains— the _____ Nevada range
9. San _____ is the city at the center of Silicon Valley.
10. Resource that first brought many people to California

California's lovely lands inspired the great naturalist John Muir to argue for the creation of national parks in California. Today, Yosemite is one of California's eight national parks.

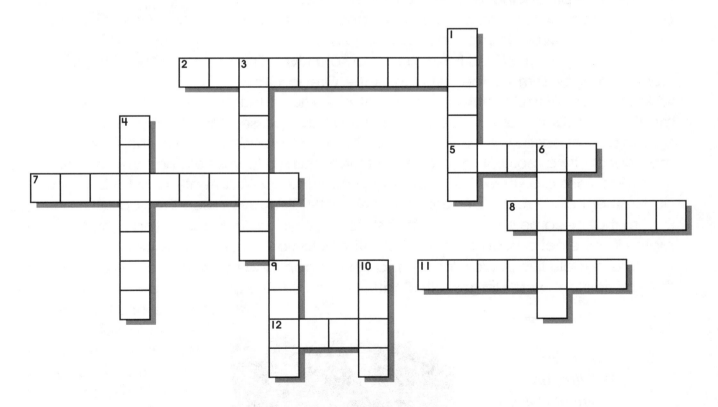

Word List

CENTRAL	GOLD	MEXICO	SIERRA
COAST	HOLLYWOOD	PEOPLE	SILICON
EARTHQUAKE	JOSE	REDWOOD	SOIL

Washington and Oregon

The beautiful volcanic Cascade Range runs through both Washington and Oregon from south to north. In 1980, Mount St. Helens in Washington erupted with huge clouds of smoke and soot, destroying houses and setting off mudslides. Most of the time, though, life is safe in the Pacific Northwest, and many people enjoy hiking and skiing on the tall mountains.

To the west of the Cascades, fertile valleys and a hilly coast get plenty of rain to water fruit and other crops. So much rain falls on Washington's Olympic Peninsula that an unusual rain forest grows there. Trees are so plentiful that Washington is called the Evergreen State, and Oregon leads the nation in producing lumber. East of the Cascades lies a high plateau where the climate is dry and temperatures are much higher in summer and lower in winter.

Between the two states flows the Columbia River. The Columbia once formed the last part of the Oregon Trail, which brought Western settlers to both states. Portland, the largest city in Oregon, lies at the mouth of the Columbia. Citizens of Portland have passed laws to ring their city with a "green belt" of parks in order to slow down the rapid spread of suburbs. Their goal is to make the central city a more attractive place to live and work, while saving farms and wildlands.

Oregonians are known for their concern for the environment—and for bringing government close to the people. In the early 1900's, they passed laws called the Oregon System that became a model for other states. The system included voting rights for women, more direct elections, and the right of citizens to vote directly on issues.

More people live in Washington than in Oregon, and many of those live in or near the Pacific Northwest's largest city, Seattle. In the Seattle area, aerospace and computer software industries are strong. The most famous person in Washington may be Bill Gates, the founder of the giant software company Microsoft.

Seattle, Washington is one of the most popular cities in the United States.

Mount Ranier in Washington

Use the word list to help you find the words about
Washington and Oregon that are hidden in the block below.
Some of the words are hidden backward or diagonally.

```
F H O S E G N A R E D A C S A C
V O R E G O N S Y S T E M U O P
B R I M O Y F E E W N O V A Y E
U E A S S G P D L A C Z S F I R
K G E N T R A I N J T T R V B A
V O T E H Z C L P M R T N O T W
A N J L M O X S C K E M L X N T
L T E E W R T D S Z E B I E E F
L R L H A R N U J F S N Q H M O
E A U T J A P M O U N T A I N S
Y I D S L B I B Y L G O D E R W
S L G T W I L D L A N D S L E U
Y X R N R E C A P S O R E A V A
C O L U M B I A R I V E R D O Q
P K A O T N T L E B N E E R G U
O L Y M P I C P E N I N S U L A
```

Word List

AEROSPACE	GREEN BELT	OREGON SYSTEM	SOFTWARE
CASCADE RANGE	MOUNT ST HELENS	OREGON TRAIL	TREES
COAST	MOUNTAINS	PORTLAND	VALLEYS
COLUMBIA RIVER	MUDSLIDES	RAIN	VOTE
GOVERNMENT	OLYMPIC PENINSULA	SEATTLE	WILDLANDS

Nevada and Utah

Nevada and Utah lie next to each other between the Sierra Nevada, on Nevada's western edge, and the Rocky Mountains, which take up the eastern half of Utah. Both states are high in altitude and have very dry, or arid, climates. The two states share an area called the Great Basin. This rocky, nearly treeless area is surrounded by mountains, but instead of a flat floor, it has ripples of ridges with valleys called "basins" between them. Streams from the mountains flow into the Great Basin only to disappear by evaporating or sinking. In northern Utah, the Great Salt Lake is all that remains of an ancient inland sea. To the south, rivers have carved the land into deep canyons and fantastic shapes.

These lands were not easy to settle, but many people settled in Nevada because of the Comstock Lode, a network of underground veins of gold and silver. That gold and silver helped the Union pay for the Civil War. The Comstock Lode was used up by the early 1900's, leaving ghost towns like Virginia City, which visitors can see today.

Utah was settled by Mormons. This religious group, led by Brigham Young, founded Salt Lake City, Utah's capital, on the edge of the Great Salt Lake. Utah remains about two-thirds Mormon. The headquarters of the church is an important place where many Americans can trace their family records. The Mormon Tabernacle Choir is also world-famous.

The people of Nevada and Utah have found ways to make a living in their harsh environment. Dams and irrigation have helped make farming and industry easier, especially in Utah. Tourists also come to Utah for winter skiing and for sightseeing in the canyon country of the south, where five national parks welcome visitors. Gambling is legal in Nevada. The casinos at Reno and Las Vegas, the two largest cities in Nevada, draw tourists from all over the United States. Nevada's capital, Carson City, is, however, a small city.

Devil's Garden in Arches National Park is one of the many unusual stone formations that can be found in Utah.

Words about Nevada and Utah have been scrambled.
Rearrange the letters and write the correct word on each line.
Use the word list if you need help.

RARIES VANEDA

_____

SAL GASEV

_____

STORUIST

_____

CYNOSAN

_____

NOUYG

_____

IGANIRVI CTYI

_____

VERSIL

_____

SABNI

_____

NIFRGMA

_____

LODG

_____

SACNOR TYIC

_____

SONMROM

_____

Word List

BASIN	FARMING	MORMONS	TOURISTS
CANYONS	GOLD	SIERRA NEVADA	VIRGINIA CITY
CARSON CITY	LAS VEGAS	SILVER	YOUNG

Idaho and Montana

The Rocky Mountains rise high in the states of Idaho and Montana. The Continental Divide runs along the southern part of the border between the two states. There, you can tell if you are in Idaho if the streams run toward the west. If the streams are running eastward, you must be in Montana!

The mountains and foothills have yielded underground treasures in both states. Silver is especially plentiful in Idaho, home of the silver mine at Coeur d' Alene. Both gold and silver were found in Montana—though today, copper, zinc, and oil are among the most profitable minerals. Above ground, the mountains provide lumber and great slopes for skiing. Sun Valley, Idaho, is one of the area's famous winter resorts. In Glacier National Park in northern Montana, you can see beautiful views of the Rocky Mountains.

The land flattens out to the west in Idaho and to the east in Montana. The valley of Idaho's Snake River has proved perfect for the state's most famous crop—potatoes. Montana's high plains produce large crops of wheat. Farmers came to these states in large numbers when the Great Northern Railroad made easy transportation possible. Montana became a state in 1889, and Idaho became one in 1890. Although these states are two of the nation's largest, their populations are among the smallest. Their capitals—Boise, Idaho, and Helena, Montana,—are small cities.

Thousands of people in both states belong to Native American tribes, and many live on large reservations there. The Native American heritage of the region is rich. It includes such famous figures as Sacajawea, who helped guide Lewis and Clark across the Rockies, and Chief Joseph, one of the last great leaders of the Nez Percé.

Read the clues about Idaho and Montana.
Then complete the puzzle using the word list on the next page.

★ Across ★

2. Name of a national park in northern Montana
4. Capital of Idaho
5. Line in the Rocky Mountains that determines which way rivers flow—the Continental ____
6. Forest product of Idaho and Montana
9. Idaho's most famous vegetable
10. Name of the railroad that made Idaho and Montana easier to settle—the Great ____

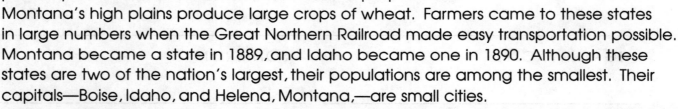

11. First word in the name of the Idaho city where a large silver mine is located

★ *Down* ★

1. Valuable mineral found in both Idaho and Montana
2. Sacajawea acted as one for the Lewis and Clark expedition.
3. Area set aside for a Native American group; there are several in Idaho and Montana
4. Animal that used to roam on the high prairies
7. Idaho river surrounded by potato farms
8. Capital of Montana
9. The Nez _____ are a Native American tribe; Chief Joseph was once their tribal leader.

Buffalo once grew fat on prairie grass in Montana's high plains.

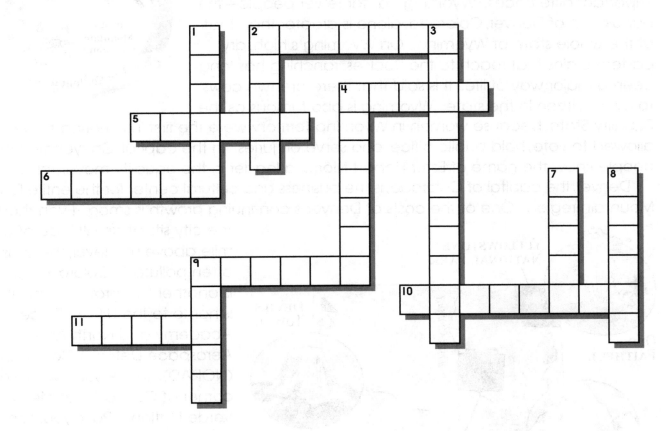

Word List

BOISE	DIVIDE	LUMBER	RESERVATION
BUFFALO	GLACIER	NORTHERN	SILVER
COEUR	GUIDE	PERCE	SNAKE
	HELENA	POTATO	

Wyoming and Colorado

Colorado has the highest average altitude in the Union, and Wyoming has the second highest. As in the other Rocky Mountain states, mining is an important industry. So is recreation. Wyoming includes the oldest American national park, Yellowstone. (Small portions of the park also falls in Montana and Idaho.) Some early pioneers passing through the region were probably scared of Yellowstone's hot springs and geysers. Beautiful mountain scenery and good skiing can be had at many other parks and resorts, such as in Jackson Hole, Wyoming, and Aspen, Colorado.

Although the two states may seem similar, there are important differences. Wyoming has far fewer people—the population of Denver, Colorado, alone is greater than that of the whole state of Wyoming. On Wyoming's high, dry eastern plains that reach to the Rockies, ranching has long been a major way of life. It is said that there are two cows to every citizen in the state. Wyoming is also famous as the Equality State, because women in Wyoming Territory were the first in America to be allowed to vote, hold public office, and serve on juries. In the capital, Cheyenne, most people know the name of Ester Hobart Morris, a leader in the equality movement.

Denver, the capital of Colorado, is the business and cultural center for the entire Rocky Mountain region. One of the costs of Denver's continuing growth is smog. Even though the city sits at an altitude of a mile above sea level, the air is often polluted. Colorado Springs is another fast-growing city. It is home to the U.S. Air Force Academy and North American Aerospace Defense Command (NORAD). In the southwestern corner of Colorado, at Mesa Verde National Park, you can see the ancient cliff dwellings of the Anasazi, a Native American people who were skilled builders.

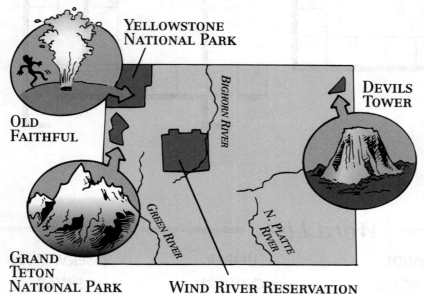

OLD FAITHFUL

YELLOWSTONE NATIONAL PARK

BIGHORN RIVER

DEVILS TOWER

GRAND TETON NATIONAL PARK

GREEN RIVER

N. PLATTE RIVER

WIND RIVER RESERVATION

Read the sentences about Wyoming and Colorado.
Then complete each sentence by filling in each blank.
Use the word list if you need help.

★ _____ River is a large Native American reservation in central Wyoming.

★ Wyoming is home to _____ and Arapaho people.

★ Esther Hobart _____ sought equality for women in Wyoming Territory.

★ America's oldest national park, located in Wyoming, is

_____ .

★ The Colorado town of _____ is famous as a ski resort.

★ The _____ were ancient Native American people who built cliff dwellings.

★ _____ has the highest average elevation in the United States.

★ Wyoming is known as the _____ State.

★ The U.S. _____ Force has an academy in Colorado Springs.

★ Wyoming has fewer _____ than Colorado.

Word List

Air	Aspen	Morris	Wind
Anasazi	Colorado	people	Yellowstone
	Equality	Shoshone	

Arizona and New Mexico

Arizona and New Mexico are located next to each other in the southwestern area of the United States. They share their southern borders with Mexico. In both states, you can find parts of the Rocky Mountains, high plains, and plateaus. In southwestern Arizona, the land dips lower into the Sonoran Desert.

People from nearly every Native American tribe on the continent come to New Mexico every year for the Intertribal Indian Ceremonial. New Mexico is a natural place for the gathering because this state and its neighbor, Arizona, include more than half the reservation land in the United States. At places like Chaco Canyon, New Mexico, you can still visit buildings created by native people hundreds of years before the arrival of Europeans. Today, many tribes continue traditions such as the Pueblo practice of building apartment-style structures of adobe bricks (made from clay mud mixed with straw). The Navajo reservation, located in northeast Arizona and part of New Mexico, is home to the nation's largest tribe. The Navajo farm and raise sheep. They practice traditional crafts including silversmithing and weaving. Discoveries of minerals on Navajo land have helped increase the tribe's income.

A significant part of the population in both states is of Mexican or Spanish heritage. The Spanish language and customs of both groups are an important part of life in cities like Santa Fe, the capital of New Mexico.

People come to Arizona and New Mexico for the dry, healthy air, and to find jobs in the growing economy of these and other warm-climate states in what is known as the Sun Belt. Arizona has had the most growth of the two states, especially in its two largest cities, Tucson and Phoenix, the capital. The natural beauty of the region is another draw. In northern Arizona, the Colorado River has carved out the spectacular Grand Canyon. Blooming deserts and New Mexico's Carlsbad Caverns present other kinds of beauty

Read the clues about Arizona and New Mexico.
Then complete the puzzle using the word list on the next page.

★ *Across* ★

3. Name of a New Mexico canyon with ancient Native American buildings
4. Nickname for the sunny region that includes New Mexico and Arizona
5. Language, other than English, that is an important part of culture in New Mexico and Arizona

10. First word of the name of the Native American ceremonial held yearly in New Mexico
11. Country bordering Arizona and New Mexico to the south
12. Tribe famous for building adobe housing
13. Largest Native American tribe in the United States

Down

1. New Mexico city that artist Georgia O'Keeffe helped make into an art center
2. Capital of Arizona
3. Name of famous caverns in New Mexico
6. The Sun Belt state with one of the fastest-growing populations in the nation
7. Animal raised by Navajo ranchers
8. Name of the canyon formed by the Colorado River
9. Name of the desert in southwest Arizona

The famous artist Georgia O'Keeffe captured the desert landscape of cities such as Taos, New Mexico.

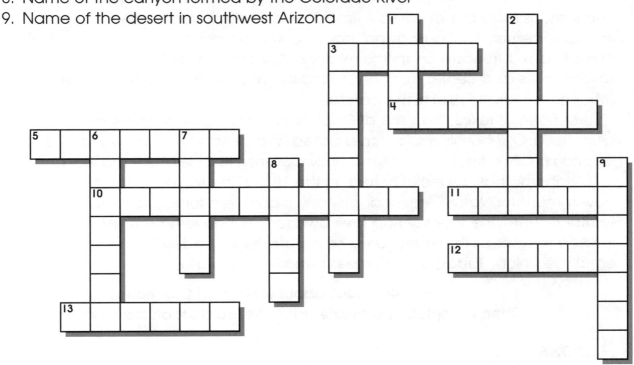

Word List

ARIZONA	GRAND	PHOENIX	SPANISH
CARLSBAD	INTERTRIBAL	PUEBLO	SUN BELT
CHACO	MEXICO	SHEEP	TAOS
	NAVAJO	SONORAN	

Texas and Oklahoma

Texas is bigger in area than any state except Alaska. Once, when Texas was part of Mexico, little moved on the vast plains that make up most of the state except cattle. Then American settlers rebelled to form their own "Lone Star" republic, and soon after, in 1845, joined the United States. People poured in to plant cotton—still the leading crop today—and to raise even more cattle. Then, in 1901, Texas's first big oil well, called Spindletop, began producing at a record rate.

Population has grown to suit the size and riches of the state. Texas is second in population only to California. Houston is the biggest city, located near the Gulf of Mexico. There, cotton is processed in mills, and oil is processed in refineries and chemical plants for easy shipping. Houston is also famous for its big, covered Astrodome stadium and for its space center. "Hello, Houston" has become a familiar phrase from astronauts on space missions. Dallas, in central Texas, serves as a center for finance and business all over the Southwest. Texas's many other cities include Austin, the capital.

Just north of Texas, the state of Oklahoma is also home to many cattle ranches and oil wells. Tulsa, Oklahoma, is sometimes called "the oil capital of the world." The state capital, Oklahoma City, attracted attention worldwide when its federal building was bombed in 1995.

Oklahoma has a special history. In the 1830's, the region was set aside by the U.S. government for Native Americans. Many tribes were forced to move to this "Indian Territory." There, the tribes set up their own forms of government. After the United States refused to accept the Indian area as a state, tribal leaders joined with white settlers to enter the Union. Today, over 60 tribes remain in the state.

Read the clues about Texas and Oklahoma.
Then complete the puzzle using the word list on the next page.

★ *Across* ★

2. The rank of Texas among the states in size and population
4. Plants where oil is processed; there are several in Houston
7. Name of the covered sports stadium in Houston
8. The nickname for Texas is the Lone _____ State.
9. Texas's biggest city
11. Valuable underground resource in both Texas and Oklahoma

Down

1. Landform in most of Texas
2. Texas's first wildly successful oil well
3. Texas city; a financial center of the Southwest
5. Most common Texas crop
6. Area set up to receive Native Americans forced from the East—Indian _____
7. Capital of Texas
10. Oklahoma city; sometimes called "the oil capital of the world"

Many people in Texas and Oklahoma still wear large ten-gallon cowboy hats—even if they are not cowboys.

Word List

ASTRODOME	**HOUSTON**	**REFINERIES**	**STAR**
AUSTIN	**OIL**	**SECOND**	**TERRITORY**
COTTON	**PLAINS**	**SPINDLETOP**	**TULSA**
DALLAS			

North Dakota and South Dakota

Some of the greatest and saddest moments in Native American history took place in the land of the Dakota, also called the Sioux. In 1874, General George Custer discovered gold on Sioux land in the Black Hills (now South Dakota). The Sioux fought the army over that land and, at the Battle of the Little Bighorn, defeated Custer and his men. Later, however, the Sioux leader Crazy Horse was killed and the government took over the Black Hills.

Sioux and other tribes still live in the Dakotas. In 1973, a group called the American Indian Movement gained publicity for Native American rights when they took over the South Dakota Sioux village of Wounded Knee. It was at Wounded Knee that the U.S. Army killed a group of Sioux men, women, and children to end resistance in 1890.

The coming of the railroad and the Homestead Act, which offered free government land, brought settlers to Dakota Territory to farm. They found the vast Great Plains, varied only by oddly shaped, eroded hills called the Badlands in the west and the Black Hills in the southwest. Today, farming and ranching remain major ways of making a living. Wheat is the chief crop in North Dakota, as is corn in South Dakota. In North Dakota, the Garrison Dam on the Missouri River has opened many thousands of acres for farming.

Oil and minerals have also been found in both Dakotas, and gold is still being taken from the Black Hills. In fact, that is the location of the largest American gold mine, the Homestake Mine. Also in the Black Hills is Mount Rushmore, a mountain carved with huge stone portraits of George Washington, Thomas Jefferson, Theodore Roosevelt, and Abraham Lincoln.

Cities in the Dakotas are not large. The capitals of both states—Bismarck, North Dakota and Pierre, South Dakota—were once trading posts on the Missouri River.

Read the clues about North Dakota and South Dakota.
Then complete the puzzle using the word list on the next page.

★ *Across* ★

1. Precious metal found in the Black Hills by General Custer
4. The capitals of both North and South Dakota are on this river.
5. Name of the South Dakota hills where Mount Rushmore is located
6. Name of the large gold mine in South Dakota
7. Name of the mountain on which the faces of four presidents are carved
10. _____ Knee, a famous Sioux village

11. Initials of the Roosevelt whose face appears on Mount Rushmore
12. Main crop in North Dakota

★ *Down* ★

1. North Dakota dam on the Missouri that has allowed more farming
2. The act that provided free government land to farmers
3. The general who made a last stand at the Little Bighorn
5. Capital of North Dakota
8. Second word in the name of the Sioux leader represented in a mountain-sized statue being carved in South Dakota
9. Initials of the state for which Pierre is the capital

Sculptors have been carving a memorial to Crazy Horse on a mountain in the Black Hills since 1948. When finished, it will be the largest sculpture in the world.

Word List

BISMARCK	GARRISON	HORSE	TR
BLACK	GOLD	MISSOURI	WHEAT
CUSTER	HOMESTAKE	RUSHMORE	WOUNDED
	HOMESTEAD	SD	

Iowa, Kansas, and Nebraska

The states of Iowa, Kansas, and Nebraska are grouped along the Missouri River at the center of the United States. In fact, Kansas contains the center of the U.S.'s 48 adjoining states. These three states are mostly flat farm country. Iowa has the richest soil and wettest climate. Nebraska and Kansas include part of the Great Plains and are a little higher and drier with harsher winters. Big thunderstorms are a feature of the weather in all these states, sometimes accompanied by tornadoes.

29th state ★ Statehood: December 28, 1846
Eastern Goldfinch
Wild Rose
IA ★ The Hawkeye State

34th state ★ Statehood: January 29, 1861
Western Meadowlark
Sunflower
KS ★ The Sunflower State

37th state ★ Statehood: March 1, 1867
Western Meadowlark
Goldenrod
NE ★ The Cornhusker State

Iowa, which is farther east, was settled earlier than the other two states and was admitted to the Union in 1846, with Des Moines as its capital. Homesteading and the expansion of the railroad brought settlers to Kansas and Nebraska. Congress decided to let the people of Kansas decide whether to enter the nation as a free or slave state. The settlers fought real battles over the issue, and the state gained the nickname, "Bleeding Kansas." At last, Kansas was admitted to the Union as a free state, with Topeka as its capital. Nebraska joined the United States after the Civil War. The nation's only unicameral (one-house) state legislature meets to make Nebraska's laws in its capital, Lincoln.

All three states are well-known for their agriculture. Iowa grows more corn and raises more hogs than any other state. It is also the place where rolled oats became the first quick breakfast cereal. The biggest cereal-making plant in the world today is in Cedar Rapids, Iowa. Kansas rivals North Dakota for the nation's largest total wheat harvest. Huge cattle ranches cover much of the land in Nebraska and Kansas.

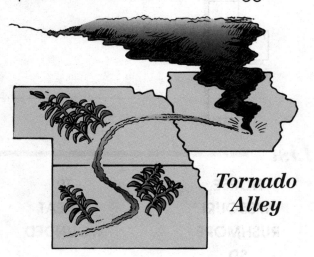

Tornado Alley

Life has been changing for families in farm states over the past few decades. Many Iowans, for example, now work at service jobs such as those in the insurance industry. Many people in Nebraska and Kansas work in manufacturing. In Wichita, Kansas's biggest city, for instance, workers put together more than half of the world's private airplanes.

Words about Iowa, Kansas, and Nebraska have been scrambled.
Rearrange the letters and write the correct word on each line.
Use the word list if you need help.

PEAKOT

_____

LACGUERRITU

_____

CENSNIARU

_____

THICAIW

_____

SELARPNAI

_____

SED NOMIES

_____

TAMARIGUUCFNN

_____

ERACLE

_____

ACRULINMEA

_____

THAEW

_____

SHEDMIONETAG

_____

NNOLCLI

_____

Word List

AGRICULTURE	DES MOINES	LINCOLN	UNICAMERAL
AIRPLANES	HOMESTEADING	MANUFACTURING	WHEAT
CEREAL	INSURANCE	TOPEKA	WICHITA

Minnesota, Wisconsin, and Michigan

Minnesota, Wisconsin, and Michigan are along the northern border of the United States, near the Great Lakes. The three states don't have many mountains, but all have some hills and plenty of streams and lakes. Minnesota claims more lakes than any other state—over 10,000!

Before the American Revolution, waterways served as highways to Native Americans, explorers, and fur traders in the Great Lakes region. Steamboats brought loads of immigrants, especially Scandinavians to Minnesota and Germans to Wisconsin. Today, the area's lakes and rivers are still major shipping routes.

Almost a hundred years ago, in Michigan, Henry Ford became the first American to make an affordable car using the assembly line. Soon Detroit became the car manufacturing capital of the world. So many people poured into the state to work in auto-related industries that the population of Michigan ballooned, and it is now about twice that of Minnesota or Wisconsin. Even smaller cities like Flint and Lansing, the capital, took part in car making. Although cars and trucks are still built in Michigan, many autoworkers have had to look for other jobs because of increasing foreign competition.

In Wisconsin, dairy farms are everywhere and cheese is an important product. So is beer, first made in this state from traditional German recipes. Milwaukee, Wisconsin's largest city, can ship its products on Lake Michigan. The capital, Madison, lies inland.

The Mississippi River begins in central Minnesota. The state's biggest cities—Minneapolis and St. Paul, the capital—lie across from each other on the river. These "Twin Cities" bustle with business and the arts, and they are home to more than a dozen colleges. The Mall of America in Bloomington also attracts many visitors.

These three states also have a wild side. They offer fishing, hunting, boating, and hiking. Isle Royale, Michigan's national park in Lake Superior, once had one of the world's largest herds of moose.

Use the word list to help you find the words about
Minnesota, Wisconsin, and Michigan that are hidden in the block below.
Some of the words are hidden backward or diagonally.

```
D F W Y D A I R Y F A R M S W Y
M I C H I G A N N O S I D A M P
A B T K V B C F E J S O U T I B
L A K E S Q F I I Z E N S A L L
L G L U C X T O E F M A O M W H
O L L A N S I N G P B N T H A I
F I S H I N G R E D L O P F U L
A P T R I S L E R O Y A L E K A
M R I L D K V O M D L N J V E T
E M O Z R J F Y A S I U X G E O
R H R O G L H E N T N E P C P S
I D T W I N C I T I E S A H X E
C K E C W G B A K U C R Q E S N
A W D X Q U V I H I M J V E D N
Z B W I S C O N S I N F R S C I
A N S E K A L T A E R G W E R M
```

Word List

ASSEMBLY LINE	FISHING	ISLE ROYALE	MICHIGAN
CAR	FORD	LAKES	MILWAUKEE
CHEESE	GERMAN	LANSING	MINNESOTA
DAIRY FARMS	GREAT LAKES	MADISON	TWIN CITIES
DETROIT	HIKING	MALL OF AMERICA	WISCONSIN

Illinois

Illinois is a busy state with farms, factories, and a successful transportation system. Illinois is the sixth most populous state.

Throughout Illinois's history, transportation routes have been the key to its success. The Mississippi River on the west and the Ohio River on the southeast border have allowed Illinois farmers and manufacturers to ship and sell goods from Canada to New Orleans and around the world. Even more valuable is the port of Chicago, one of the largest on the Great Lakes, with easy shipping routes eastward. The railroads gave Illinois a big economic boost as they brought grain and cattle from the West to Chicago for sale to eastern cities. Today, interstate truck routes and airplanes have joined the transportation web.

The city of Chicago, third largest in the nation after New York and Los Angeles, is a very exciting place. The first skyscraper was built there, and today, Chicago is home to the tallest building in the nation, the Sears Tower. Inside some of the skyscrapers, bankers are at work—this is the financial center of the Midwest. Once, poet Carl Sandburg called Chicago "hog butcher to the world." The slaughterhouses may have moved, but the Chicago Board of Trade remains the world's largest market for trading in grain and meat. O'Hare International Airport is among the busiest in the world. Culture in Chicago is lively, too. The city hums with jazz and the blues. The Art Institute of Chicago houses one of the finest art collections in the nation. And the Chicago Bulls basketball team is one of the nation's most popular.

There is a quieter side of Illinois south of Chicago. Most of the flat, fertile plains are farmland. Springfield, the state capital, sits in the middle of the state. There, you can visit memorials to Abraham Lincoln, perhaps the state's most famous citizen. To the south are hilly areas with woods and lakes.

Chicago is called the Windy City for a good reason!

30

Words about Illinois have been scrambled.
Rearrange the letters and write the correct word on each line.
Use the word list if you need help.

SPERASCKYR

_____

DARRLOAIS

_____

ZAJZ

_____

SPOTRAINTOTNAR

_____

IRDSNEGPFIL

_____

IOHO RIERV

_____

SLUBL

_____

COLINNL

_____

FLARDAMN

_____

COGHACI

_____

RSEAS REWTO

_____

INARG

_____

Word List

BULLS	GRAIN	OHIO RIVER	SKYSCRAPER
CHICAGO	JAZZ	RAILROADS	SPRINGFIELD
FARMLAND	LINCOLN	SEARS TOWER	TRANSPORTATION

Indiana and Ohio

Soon after the Revolutionary War, Americans began to move across the Appalachian Mountains to the Ohio River valley and the land between it and the Great Lakes. This piece of land was soon made into states according to the Northwest Ordinance. This law, passed by Congress, allowed new states to enter the Union as equals of the original states if they met certain conditions. In 1803, Ohio was the first state created under these rules; land just to the west of Ohio became the state of Indiana.

19th state ★ Statehood: December 11, 1816
Cardinal
Peony
IN ★ The Hoosier State

Ohio grew in population more quickly than Indiana, and today, Ohio is full of cities both large and small. The largest cities in these two states were founded near water transportation. Cleveland became an industrial giant at the northern border of Ohio on Lake Erie, and Cincinnati grew as a major shipping point for goods on the Ohio River to the south. In Indiana, the city of Gary on Lake Michigan was closely linked with Chicago's trade.

17th state ★ Statehood: March 1, 1803
Cardinal
Scarlet Carnation
OH ★ The Buckeye State

Most land in Ohio and Indiana was scraped flat by glaciers thousands of years ago and is good for farming. In the east and south of Ohio, the Appalachian Plateau rises as a hilly region with steep ravines. Much of this land is covered with forests, and coal and oil are found there. Hills continue along the Ohio River at the southern borders of Ohio and Indiana. Huge salt deposits lie near Lake Erie, and beautiful limestone is quarried in Indiana. Service industries and manufacturing, such as steelmaking, are very important to both Indiana and Ohio.

Indianapolis, the capital and largest city of Indiana, is famous for its Indianapolis 500 auto race. Ohio State University, located in Columbus—the capital and largest city in Ohio—draws students and football fans to its large campus. The city of Cleveland, Ohio, has built a new theater district to draw visitors downtown.

OHIO
OIL COAL
SALT
INDIANA
INDY 500
LIMESTONE

Use the word list to help you find the words about Indiana
and Ohio that are hidden in the block below.
Some of the words are hidden backward or diagonally.

```
F  B  M  D  N  A  L  E  V  E  L  C  A  B  O  A
C  A  L  R  T  P  C  O  L  U  M  B  U  S  U  G
I  S  I  L  O  P  A  N  A  I  D  N  I  T  O  N
N  E  F  S  R  A  T  Z  O  A  T  H  O  V  Q  I
C  N  A  F  D  L  K  R  W  S  T  R  S  I  S  R
I  A  R  O  I  A  K  M  F  U  A  I  E  T  R  U
N  G  M  L  N  C  O  I  L  C  Z  T  S  E  M  T
N  I  I  I  T  A  H  H  C  E  R  E  E  O  I  E
A  H  N  O  N  I  I  I  K  P  R  I  D  R  T  C
T  C  G  Y  C  A  O  H  I  O  R  I  V  E  R  A
I  I  I  I  A  E  N  S  W  F  J  O  O  N  E  I
A  M  W  M  R  G  T  X  U  V  N  T  N  K  C  U
Y  E  D  E  X  Y  A  B  T  O  R  O  C  A  N  N
L  K  T  R  J  X  T  I  N  C  U  Z  O  L  P  A
V  A  Q  L  I  M  E  S  T  O  N  E  A  G  O  M
W  L  A  I  N  D  U  S  T  R  I  A  L  D  M  S
```

Word List

APPALACHIAN	COLUMBUS	INDUSTRIAL	ORDINANCE
AUTO RACE	FARMING	LAKE ERIE	OHIO RIVER
CINCINNATI	FORESTS	LAKE MICHIGAN	OHIO STATE
CLEVELAND	GARY	LIMESTONE	OIL
COAL	INDIANAPOLIS	MANUFACTURING	WATER

Pennsylvania

The English Quaker William Penn founded the colony of Pennsylvania, which means "Penn's Woods." He invited people from many parts of Europe to come and farm peacefully together, and he tried to treat the Native Americans fairly. Today, Pennsylvania is the nation's fifth largest state in population. Even though the state has so many people, plenty of countryside remains for hiking, skiing, and hunting in state parks and reserves. In the middle of Pennsylvania, the small city of Harrisburg serves as the state's capital.

The state includes a flat coastal plains area, a higher lowland called the Piedmont, and then the Appalachian Mountains, also called the Alleghenies in this state. On the western side of the state, the Appalachian Plateau, a hilly region, descends to the Great Lakes area and across the border with Ohio. The richest land is in the southeast, "Pennsylvania Dutch" country. The Dutch are really "Deutsch," or Germans, whose ancestors responded to advertisements made in Europe by Penn. Pennsylvania is a leader in dairy products, chickens, eggs, apples, mushrooms—and Christmas trees!

The state has two major cities, Philadelphia in the east and Pittsburgh in the west. Philadelphia, the largest, was actually planned by William Penn. It is still a port and a commercial center, as he meant it to be, but now it is one of the world's great cities. Many of the nation's largest corporations have headquarters in the city. Some of the great events in U.S. history took place here, including the writing of the Declaration of Independence and the Constitution. Today, you can visit the sites of these events and others within Independence National Historic Park.

Pittsburgh grew up where the Allegheny and Monongahela Rivers meet to form the Ohio River. The city sits atop underground coalfields that, along with iron ore, built the city as a steelmaker. Today, some steel is still made in the area, but the city's economy is now based on services, technology, and education (colleges and universities).

Read the clues about Pennsylvania.
Then complete the puzzle using the word list on the next page.

★ Across ★

2. Pennsylvania's largest city
5. Name of the national historic park where you can see famous Philadelphia buildings
8. The founder of Pennsylvania was one.
9. Pittsburgh grew up as a maker of this.
10. Pennsylvania's chief western city

11. Term for milk and milk products; Pennsylvania produces a lot

Down

1. River that joins the Monongahela to form the Ohio River
3. Capital of Pennsylvania
4. *Pennsylvania* means "Penn's _____."
6. The "Pennsylvania Dutch" are really of this ethnic background.
7. Founder of the colony of Pennsylvania

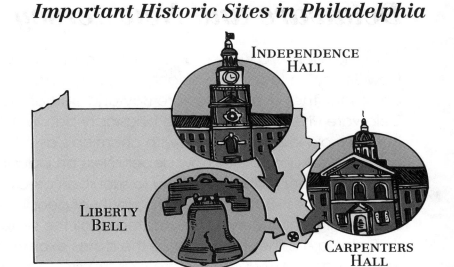

Important Historic Sites in Philadelphia

INDEPENDENCE HALL

LIBERTY BELL

CARPENTERS HALL

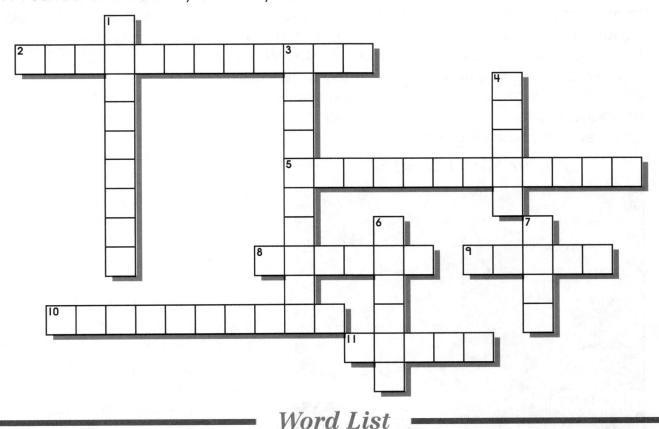

Word List

ALLEGHENY	HARRISBURG	PHILADELPHIA	STEEL
DAIRY	INDEPENDENCE	PITTSBURGH	WOODS
GERMAN	PENN	QUAKER	

Delaware and New Jersey

"What did Dela ware?" asks the old song. "She wore a New Jersey." In fact, these neighboring states have a lot in common. They share Delaware Bay and part of the Delaware River, which form the boundary between them. Both are old industrial states, with chemicals as a top product. Yet both states now depend less on industry, and more of the population is moving to suburban areas and to jobs in services. Both states have plenty of people—New Jersey is the most densely populated of all the states.

Statehood: December 7, 1787
1st state
Blue Hen Chicken
Peach Blossom
DE ★ The First State

Delaware is the smallest of all the states except for Rhode Island. In 1787, Delaware was the first to ratify the U.S. Constitution, and so became the first state, with Dover as its capital. Much of southern Delaware remains quiet farm country, where chickens are the main product. Rehoboth, a town on the Atlantic, is a good place to enjoy the waves. Northern Delaware is much busier. Wilmington, at the mouth of the Delaware River, is the state's chief city. State laws give tax advantages to corporations, so many have located their headquarters there. DuPont has headed the list of chemical companies in Delaware for a very long time. Today, it is Delaware's largest employer.

Statehood: December 18, 1787
3rd state
Eastern Goldfinch
Purple Violet
NJ ★ The Garden State

Major Water Routes

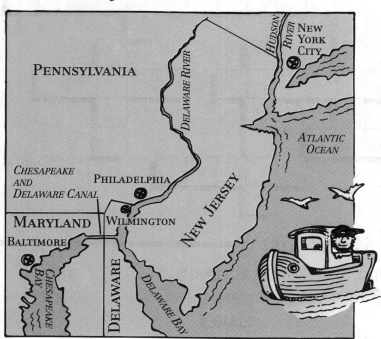

New Jersey lies between the giant cities of Philadelphia and New York, and much of its industry grew along that line. Trenton, the capital, sits midway along this line on the Delaware River. New Jersey farms supply many of the needs of the people of New York City and of the nation. Most farmland is in the southern part of the state. Atlantic City, on the coast, has become famous for casino gambling. Hills and mountains in New Jersey's northwest section offer good places to ski and hike.

Use the word list to help you find the words about
Delaware and New Jersey that are hidden in the block below.
Some of the words are hidden backward or diagonally.

```
A Z W I L M I N G T O N L S P D
T C O N S T I T U T I O N E L Z
L S W Q B M E L L R U Y P R D X
A Y E S R E J W E N G T E V E L
N D P V N F B V T A J V C I L A
T E F N Z I S N T B I K H C A I
I L H U M R O I D R X R I E W R
C A X C O P U G E U C H C S A T
C W N G U Q F R C B Y O K E R S
I A O D N M A A S U F R E E E U
T R U E T W E E X S M B N J B D
Y E K F A R M S I K S T S P A N
B I H L I D P K C L O B C R Y I
H U E T N J S W L N G R E V O D
I D C I S A D I J L K O Z Q D T
O A V L W C H E M I C A L S A I
```

Word List

ATLANTIC CITY	DELAWARE BAY	HIKE	SERVICES
CHEMICALS	DELAWARE RIVER	HILLS	SKI
CHICKENS	DOVER	INDUSTRIAL	SUBURBAN
CONSTITUTION	DUPONT	MOUNTAINS	TRENTON
DELAWARE	FARMS	NEW JERSEY	WILMINGTON

New York

They call it the Big Apple. It's New York City, the biggest city in the United States and the cornerstone of a big, busy state. After the Revolutionary War, New York City served as the first capital of the new nation. The large harbor at New York City invited trade from the beginning, and it became even more important after the Erie Canal was opened in the 1820's. The canal ran eastward from Buffalo on the shore of Lake Erie to Albany, the state capital, located on the Hudson River. The canal, then the railroad, and then trucks took increasing loads of goods from the middle of the country via Great Lakes ports to New York City. There, goods were bought, sold, and shipped all over the country and the world. A chain of industrial cities grew up along this water and railroad route, including Buffalo, Rochester, Syracuse, Utica, and others.

Today, although heavy industries like steel have closed many of their plants, New York remains a leading state in manufacturing, wholesale trade, communication, and finance. Some leading products are books and magazines—New York is the nation's chief publishing city. Another leading industry is clothing. And at the Stock Exchange on Wall Street in New York City, you can see every kind of American business being traded, and feel the pulse of the American economy as a whole.

Tourism is also a big business in New York. People come to the Big Apple for theater, famous art museums, music, shopping, and fun. They also come to see historical sites such as the Statue of Liberty in New York Harbor and Ellis Island, where many immigrants first arrived in the United States. The state of New York also includes farmland and beautiful natural spots away from the cities. There are several thousand lakes in New York, including Lake Ontario, which is one of the largest.

**Read the clues about New York.
Then complete the puzzle using the word list on the next page.**

★ Across ★

1. From the beginning, this haven for ships helped New York City trade.
3. Product of heavy industry; made less than in the past in New York
6. One of New York's largest lakes, along with Lake Erie
7. Name of forested mountains in the northeastern part of New York
8. Type of exchange on Wall Street
10. Name of the canal between Buffalo and Albany
12. One of the major cities at the western end of the canal

Down

2. Form of transportation built alongside the Erie Canal route
3. One of the industrial cities that developed because of the Erie Canal
4. The Statue of _____ stands in New York Harbor.
5. You read these; many are made in New York
7. Nickname for New York City—the Big _____
9. Capital of New York
11. Name of the island where many immigrants first landed

New York's Natural Attractions

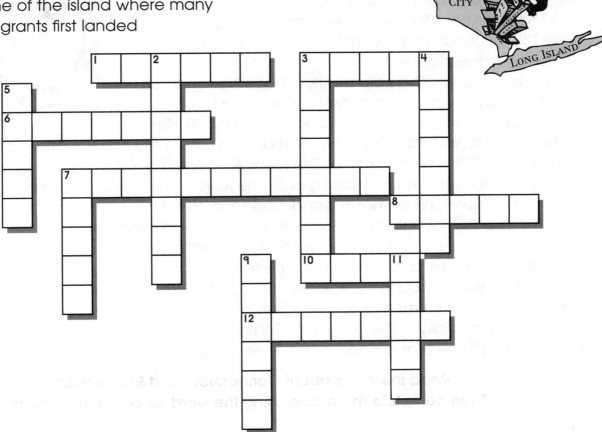

Word List

ADIRONDACKS	BOOKS	HARBOR	STEEL
ALBANY	BUFFALO	LIBERTY	STOCK
APPLE	ELLIS	ONTARIO	SYRACUSE
	ERIE	RAILROAD	

Connecticut and Rhode Island

Both Connecticut and Rhode Island have rich colonial histories. Connecticut's first constitution, the Fundamental Orders, set rules under which the colony governed itself. The orders served as one model for the U.S. Constitution. Rhode Island, the nation's smallest state, was founded by people seeking religious freedom from the Puritans in Massachusetts. Rhode Island became the first colony to formally declare independence from Britain.

Both states have prospered because of their Atlantic coastlines. Connecticut's long, sheltered coast along Long Island Sound afforded good harbors such as New London and Mystic, famous for shipbuilding and whaling in the early 1800's. Today, many commuters to New York live in southern Connecticut, in towns like Stamford.

Rhode Island's harbors are mostly in huge Narragansett Bay. Newport, on an island in the bay, has long been famous as a resort town and has boat races and music festivals. Today, you can visit Newport mansions where the rich vacationed beginning in the mid-1700's. The port city of Providence, on the mainland, is the state capital. Many people there work at making costume jewelry. Long ago, Samuel Slater built the nation's first fabric mill in Rhode Island, and soon all New England was humming with such mills. Today, though, most Rhode Islanders work in service jobs.

Industry remains important in Connecticut, which is a large producer of aircraft engines, submarines, and helicopters. The fertile Connecticut River valley cuts a farming belt north to south through the middle of the state. Hartford, the capital, sits on the river. The headquarters for many insurance firms are located there. Much of the rest of the state is hilly, especially in the northwest. That part of the Appalachian highlands is called the Berkshires, known as a good place to see autumn leaves.

Read the clues about Connecticut and Rhode Island.
Then complete the puzzle using the word list on the next page.

★ Across ★

2. Capital of Connecticut
3. Kind of jewelry made in Providence
6. Waterway off Connecticut's south shore—the Long Island _____
8. Connecticut's early constitution—the _____ Orders
11. Name of Rhode Island's very large bay

12. Connecticut leads in producing this kind of engine.

Famous Universities in Connecticut and Rhode Island

★ Down ★

1. Capital of Rhode Island
4. Fancy house; you can visit old ones in Newport
5. Mountains in Connecticut's northwest
6. Many people who live in this Connecticut town commute to New York for work.
7. Many large companies in this business are headquartered in Hartford.
9. Newport is located on one of these.
10. Last name of the man who built the first fabric mill in New England

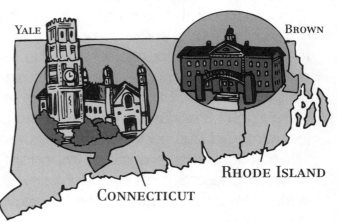

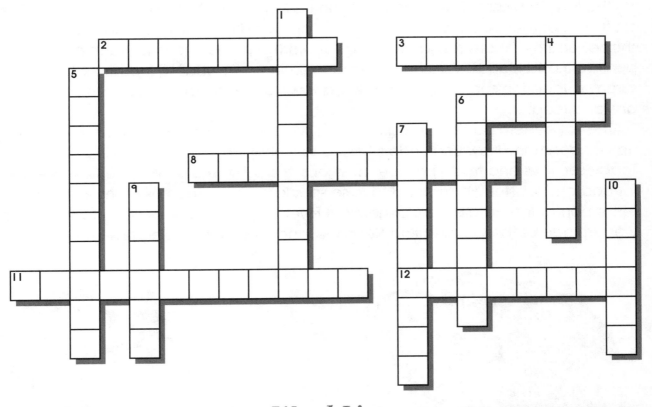

Word List

AIRCRAFT	HARTFORD	MANSION	SLATER
BERKSHIRES	INSURANCE	NARRAGANSETT	SOUND
COSTUME	ISLAND	PROVIDENCE	STAMFORD
FUNDAMENTAL			

Massachusetts

Massachusetts has a history full of firsts. It was the first of the colonies to enjoy democracy and town meetings, the first to sponsor public schools, the first to have a college and a library, and the first to act against the British in the Revolutionary War. Many reminders of the state's rich history are available to the public today, including Old Sturbridge Village, a re-creation of a typical New England town in the 1830s.

Massachusetts remains an important state despite its small size. Boston, the capital of Massachusetts, is an important city for the New England region and the rest of the nation. Massachusetts is home to many of the nation's finest colleges, including Harvard University—the first university to be founded in the United States. High-tech computer and electronics businesses have settled near such research institutions as the Massachusetts Institute of Technology (MIT).

The land in Massachusetts is low in the east and rises toward the west. From the southeast corner of the state, the sandy Cape Cod peninsula stretches out in a hook shape. South of it are the large islands of Martha's Vineyard and Nantucket. While the peninsula and islands were once home to fishing and whaling industries, today they are summer vacation spots. Provincetown, a town at the tip of the Cape, is known for its arts and theater.

The flat eastern part of the state is thickly populated, but the soil is sandy and rocky. It's no wonder many New Englanders turned to fishing or manufacturing instead of farming. Today, services and trade provide most jobs, though there is still some fishing—chiefly for cod and lobster. Farms tend to raise specialty crops, such as cranberries. The most fertile part of the state is the Connecticut River valley, which runs north to south. On the western side of the Connecticut River, the land rises to the rolling hills of the Berkshires.

Visitors can relive history at Plymoth Plantation, a re-creation of a 1627 Pilgrim village in Plymouth, Massachusetts.

Words about Massachusetts have been scrambled.
Rearrange the letters and write the correct word on each line.
Use the word list if you need help.

RAHRDAV

_____

HFGNISI

_____

PEAC DOC

_____

BKSHERIERS

_____

WORTNOVIPENC

_____

WONT NIEGMSET

_____

LUBCIP OLOSSCH

_____

BORETLS

_____

ATACINOV

_____

TUNCANTEK

_____

RBISCANERER

_____

STONOB

_____

Word List

BERKSHIRES	CRANBERRIES	LOBSTER	PUBLIC SCHOOLS
BOSTON	FISHING	NANTUCKET	TOWN MEETINGS
CAPE COD	HARVARD	PROVINCETOWN	VACATION

New Hampshire, Vermont, and Maine

New Hampshire, Vermont, and Maine make up the northeastern corner of the United States. They are all well known for their beautiful forests and mountains, and for their long, snowy winters attractive to skiers. Tourism is a major business in all three states. Though the states all have similar terrain, each has its own character.

New Hampshire was one of the original thirteen colonies. Its capital, Concord, is especially busy every four years because the state hosts the earliest presidential primary election in the nation. New Hampshire is also well known for its unusual tax laws—it has no state income tax or state sales tax. That is because most citizens of the state are conservative—they want to limit the powers of government.

Vermont was an area in dispute between New York and New Hampshire before Vermonters decided to form their own independent republic in 1777. Vermont helped fight the British in the American Revolution and afterward joined the Union as the fourteenth state. Vermont has no seacoast, though its largest city, Burlington, is on Lake Champlain. Montpelier, the capital, is in the center of the state. Vermont shares deposits of granite and marble with New Hampshire. Politically, however, the state is liberal—most Vermonters want government to help solve problems.

The area that is known as Maine once belonged to Massachusetts, but it became a state on its own in 1820. Lumber industries are the major source of income. Portland is the largest city in Maine. In fact, most people live in the southwestern part of the state. L.L. Bean, the clothing and outdoor outfitter whose catalogs reach the whole country, is located in Freeport. North of the capital, Augusta, the population thins. Potato farms fill some northern counties. There are fewer fishermen along the coast than in the past, but the beauty of the area still draws many visitors.

Words about New Hampshire, Vermont, and Maine
have been scrambled. Rearrange the letters and write the
correct word on each line. Use the word list if you need help.

STERFOS

_____

TIOUMRS

_____

REBALLI

_____

CROONCD

_____

RISESK

_____

BLUPERIC

_____

RULMEB

_____

IMAPACHLN

_____

SMNOIUANT

_____

PEOERRTF

_____

TELNIECO

_____

TRAEING

_____

Word List

CHAMPLAIN	FORESTS	LIBERAL	REPUBLIC
CONCORD	FREEPORT	LUMBER	SKIERS
ELECTION	GRANITE	MOUNTAINS	TOURISM

Tennessee, Kentucky, and West Virginia

The Appalachian Mountains extend all the way from Maine to Georgia. They take up much of the land of Tennessee, Kentucky, and West Virginia. In fact, West Virginia is the most mountainous state east of the Rockies. You can enjoy the beauty of these mountains in Great Smoky Mountains National Park in Tennessee and North Carolina.

Settlement of these areas began when the earliest pioneers, including Daniel Boone, crossed the mountains from the East. Kentucky and Tennessee became states in the 1790's. West Virginia was then part of the state of Virginia. It did not become a state until the Civil War, when people in this region decided not to secede from, or leave, the Union with the rest of Virginia.

The beautiful Appalachians have yielded plentiful coal and wood products, but they are hard to farm, and miners in the mountains have faced bad conditions and long periods without work. Still, the mountain people have a proud cultural heritage including folk music, crafts, and stories.

Manufacturing has become the main source of income in all three states. Tourists also enjoy the mountains and come through historic towns like the capitals—Charleston, West Virginia; Frankfort, Kentucky; or Nashville, Tennessee. Some traditional ways of making a living are still thriving. In Kentucky, Thoroughbred horses are still raised and sold around the world from the Bluegrass region, and bourbon whiskey continues to be made. Tennessee has benefited from the dam and lake system created by the national Tennessee Valley Authority (TVA) to create inexpensive electricity, a project begun in the 1930's. Yet cotton still grows as it did a hundred years ago in eastern Tennessee. The first trade highways for these states were the Ohio and Mississippi Rivers, which continue to carry goods today.

Read the clues about Tennessee, Kentucky, and West Virginia.
Then complete the puzzle using the word list on the next page.

★ Across ★

1. Crop traditionally grown in eastern Tennessee

2. Kind of racehorse raised in Kentucky
4. First name of an early Kentucky pioneer
5. Nashville is called the capital of country _____.
6. Economic activity that brings most money to Kentucky, West Virginia, and Tennessee
9. Capital of Kentucky
10. The Great _____ Mountains National Park lies partly in Tennessee.

★ Down ★

1. Capital of West Virginia
2. Initials of the government system of dams and lakes along the Tennessee River
3. Kind of grass; name of Kentucky's horse country
7. West Virginia became a state after it refused to leave the _____ in the Civil War.
8. Mineral most mined in the Appalachian Mountains

The Appalachians, a popular area with tourists, are known for coal mining.

Nashville, Tennessee, is the capital of country music.

Word List

BLUEGRASS	COTTON	MANUFACTURING	THOROUGHBRED
CHARLESTON	DANIEL	MUSIC	TVA
COAL	FRANKFORT	SMOKY	UNION

Mississippi and Louisiana

Mississippi and Louisiana sit on either side of the Mississippi River as it flows to its end in the Gulf of Mexico. In these states, you can relive the history of the Deep South— and see how the South has changed. Mississippi's first very profitable crop was cotton, and cotton remains "king" of agriculture in the state today. That is because the state is perfectly suited to big cotton farms—the land is flat and fertile, the temperature warm all year, and rainfall plentiful. Today, however, most Mississippians work in services or manufacturing rather than agriculture. A small number of workers and machinery now do the farm work once done by slaves under the old plantation system. Near Natchez, you can see historic mansions built by plantation owners before the Civil War. And at Vicksburg, a port on the Mississippi, you can visit the site of the Civil War battle that marked a turning point in the war in favor of the Union.

Mississippi includes the forested Piney Woods region, where trees are cut down to make paper, turpentine, and other products. Along the Gulf Coast, shrimping and fishing boats are at work. The capital, Jackson, lies in the middle of the state and is the largest city.

Louisiana is famous throughout the world, mostly because of the colorful city of New Orleans. Louisiana's heritage is largely French—it was the cultural center of the Louisiana Purchase. The economic strength of the state was first based on its control of trade at the mouth of the Mississippi. River barges and oceangoing vessels still churn the river waters between Baton Rouge, the capital, and New Orleans. Trade continues to be the most important business in the state, followed closely by tourism. People flock to New Orleans to hear good jazz in the city where it was born, and to enjoy delicious foods—such as soup called gumbo—that combine French and American flavors. Many tourists also come to the city each year for Mardi Gras, New Orleans's biggest holiday, which is celebrated with parades and fun costumes.

Read the clues about Mississippi and Louisiana.
Then complete the puzzle using the word list on the next page.

★ Across ★

2. Slave labor was used to support this kind of large farm.
4. Second word in the name of New Orleans's famous holiday
6. Mississippi's top economic activity today, along with manufacturing

7. A forested area of Mississippi is called the _____ Woods region.
9. What parading people wear at Mardi Gras
10. French and American soup served in New Orleans
11. Near this city, you can see mansions from before the Civil War.
12. Body of water into which the Mississippi flows— _____ of Mexico

★ Down ★

1. Capital of Mississippi
3. A liquid product gained from Mississippi trees
5. Location of a major Civil War battle in Mississippi
6. Edible sea animal harvested from the Gulf of Mexico, along with fish
8. Nation that put its cultural stamp on New Orleans

Scenes from Mississippi and Louisiana

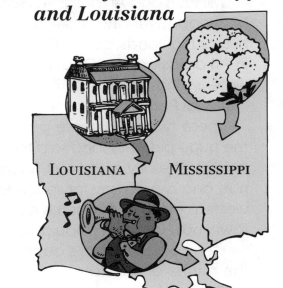

LOUISIANA   MISSISSIPPI

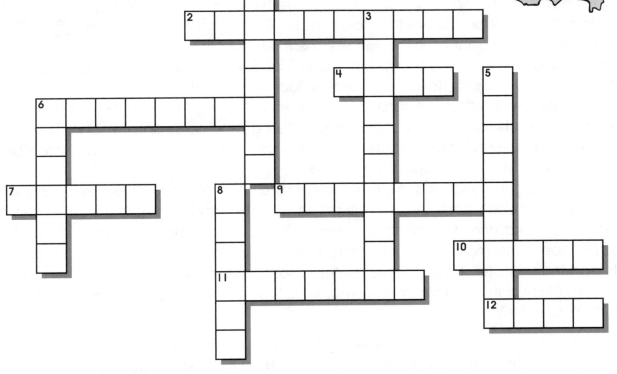

Word List

COSTUMES	GUMBO	PINEY	SHRIMP
FRANCE	JACKSON	PLANTATION	TURPENTINE
GRAS	NATCHEZ	SERVICES	VICKSBURG
GULF			

Missouri and Arkansas

Missouri and Arkansas lie along the western side of the Mississippi River and share a range of low mountains and hills, or highlands, called the Ozarks. South of the Ozarks in Arkansas are the Ouachita Mountains. They are full of water springs, including 47 hot ones at beautiful Hot Springs National Park.

These two states were part of the Louisiana Purchase, the huge piece of land sold to the United States by France in 1803. The city of St. Louis, Missouri, became a midwestern hub and a gateway for settlement of the West. At the far western edge of Missouri is Kansas City. This former cow town, now larger in population than St. Louis, still has a western look. Missouri's capital, small Jefferson City, lies in the center of the state.

Both states also have a foot in the southern region. During the Civil War, citizens from both states fought on both sides of the conflict, although Arkansas left the Union and Missouri did not. Much later, in the 1950's, Arkansas was in the spotlight during the struggle for civil rights. The United States Supreme Court ruled that public schools must accept students without regard to their race. In many places across the South, including Arkansas, black and white students had been attending separate schools. After the court ruling, several black students braved angry crowds to enroll at Central High School in Little Rock, the state capital, for the first time.

In the past, farming was the main way of life in both states. It remains a chief industry in Missouri, where nearly every crop grows. Manufacturing is now the most important industry in Arkansas. People there make a living processing food, making electrical appliances, and making paper—among other things. The Wal-Mart chain of stores got its start in the state. Today, however, Arkansas may be most famous as the birthplace of William (Bill) Clinton, a former governor who was elected president of the United States in 1992 and 1996.

Read the clues about Missouri and Arkansas.
Then complete the puzzle using the word list on the next page.

★ Across ★

2. Missouri's capital—_____ City
4. He was an Arkansas governor before he became a U.S. president.
7. Economic activity now more important than farming in Arkansas

10. First word in the name of Arkansas's capital
11. Arkansas has the only mine for these in the nation.

Down

1. Name of the Little Rock high school spotlighted in the Civil Rights era
3. Still a major economic activity in Missouri
5. Both Arkansas and Missouri were part of the _____ Purchase.
6. Mountains in southern Arkansas
8. Name of the monument arch in St. Louis
9. Popular dessert food introduced at the 1904 St. Louis World's Fair—_____ cream

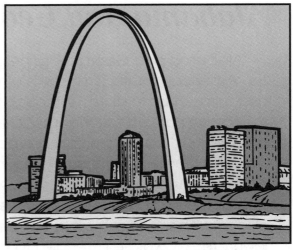

The Gateway Arch in St. Louis, Missouri, reminds people of the city's history as a gateway for settlement of the West.

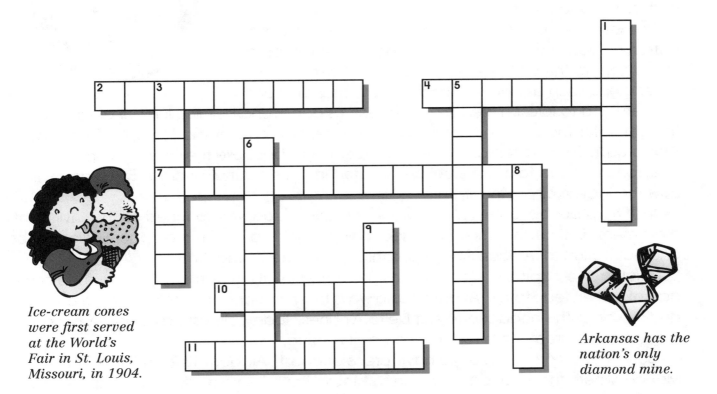

Ice-cream cones were first served at the World's Fair in St. Louis, Missouri, in 1904.

Arkansas has the nation's only diamond mine.

Word List

CENTRAL   FARMING   JEFFERSON   MANUFACTURING
CLINTON   GATEWAY   LITTLE   OUACHITA
DIAMONDS   ICE   LOUISIANA

Alabama and Georgia

Alabama and Georgia are neighbors in the heart of the American South. Coastal plains cover the southern two-thirds of both states, although the land rises in a rolling area called the Piedmont. North of the Piedmont are hills and mountains that are part of the Appalachians. Settlers quickly found that the Piedmont and plains were prime cotton-growing lands. Georgia, one of the original thirteen colonies, developed an economy based on the plantation system and slave labor. This way of life extended to the area that became Alabama. Both states were part of the Confederacy during the Civil War. There have been many changes in both states since that time.

Boll weevils—insects that eat cotton crops—destroyed cotton harvests during the 1920's. Today, there is even a monument to the boll weevil in Alabama! Farmers tried other crops, such as peanuts, and some former farmland was returned to forest. Forest products such as paper and building lumber are important to both states today. Manufacturing and services now employ most people. Birmingham, Alabama, is a major iron and steel producer, partly because the coal, iron ore, and limestone needed to make steel are located in the surrounding area. Birmingham is now the largest city in the state.

In 1955, a bus boycott in Montgomery, Alabama's capital, touched off the Civil Rights movement. In time, that movement led to voting rights and to more opportunities in jobs and education for African Americans throughout the United States.

Atlanta, the capital of Georgia, has become the urban center of the southeastern part of the United States. Atlanta has always been important as a transportation hub and serves as the headquarters of Delta Air Lines. Today, almost half of all Georgians live within the greater metropolitan area of Atlanta.

Both Alabama and Georgia have areas of coast. Alabama's is on the Gulf of Mexico, where fishing boasts come in to Mobile Bay. Georgia's Atlantic coast attracts tourists, as does the wildlife refuge in the Okefenokee Swamp.

52

Words about Alabama and Georgia have been scrambled.
Rearrange the letters and write the correct word on each line.
Use the word list if you need help.

TALANTA

_____

SEFORT

_____

ELEST

_____

CASPAHALAPIN

_____

GONERTYMOM

_____

FILEDILW

_____

TAPNLOAINT

_____

AFEEDORNCCY

_____

GAMRIMINBH

_____

DOEMIPNT

_____

VICLI SHRIGT

_____

TOCNOT

_____

Word List

APPALACHIANS	CIVIL RIGHTS	FOREST	PLANTATION
ATLANTA	CONFEDERACY	MONTGOMERY	STEEL
BIRMINGHAM	COTTON	PIEDMONT	WILDLIFE

Florida

What is the most popular single-attraction tourist destination in the world? You can probably guess the answer—Disney World in Florida. Florida also has so many other attractions that it's no wonder tourism is the state's top moneymaker.

Part of Florida's appeal is its climate and location. The state is a large peninsula that extends southward into the Atlantic Ocean. Attached to the peninsula is a northwestern panhandle of Gulf Coast land where Tallahassee, the state capital, lies. Because of its shape, Florida has an enormous continuous coastline that attracts people to its beaches and boat docks. Florida's climate is warm all year. In the far southern part of the state, including many small islands called the Florida Keys, the climate is tropical, which means it changes little with the seasons. Even in northern Florida, winter temperatures rarely fall below freezing. However, Florida is often in the path of hurricanes.

Florida caught the eye of Europeans in the early 1500's. Spain established the first permanent settlement in North America at St. Augustine, on the northeast coast. The Spanish first grew oranges in Florida; today, citrus fruits are the state's most valuable crop. Beginning in the 1800's, Florida became a destination for "snowbirds," people escaping from winter in the northeastern states. Others come to Florida to retire. Large communities of retired people have increased the population of cities like St. Petersburg. Florida has also become home to Hispanic people from south of the U.S. border, including many Cubans.

Visitors to Florida are likely to stop in the Orlando area, where there are many theme parks, including Universal Studios and Sea World. East of Orlando on the coast is the Kennedy Space Center at Cape Canaveral.

Read the clues about Florida.
Then complete the puzzle using the word list on the next page.

★ *Across* ★

1. Country that established the first permanent settlement in North America
5. Capital of Florida
7. Florida city where many theme parks are located
8. Name of islands below the southern tip of the Florida peninsula
9. People who winter in Florida's warm climate are given this nickname.
10. Severe kind of storm that sometimes blasts Florida
11. The northwestern Gulf Coast strip of Florida is shaped like a _____ handle.

Down

1. Universal _____ is a theme park in Florida.
2. Name of the "World" that is the world's top tourist destination; in Florida
3. Name of the Florida cape where spacecraft are launched into space
4. Florida city with many retired people: St. _____
6. Chief economic activity in Florida
9. Kind of land within Everglades National Park

At Everglades National Park, you can take an airboat through swampland to see pelicans, alligators, and other creatures.

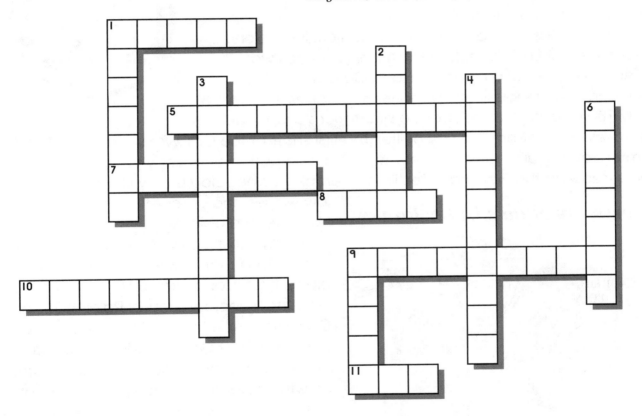

Word List

CANAVERAL	ORLANDO	SNOWBIRDS	SWAMP
DISNEY	PAN	SPAIN	TALLAHASSEE
HURRICANE	PETERSBURG	STUDIOS	TOURISM
KEYS			

North Carolina and South Carolina

NC ★ The Tar Heel State

Both the Carolinas have miles and miles of beaches. In both states, the wide coastal plain ends at the slightly higher, rolling red-clay country called the Piedmont. The Piedmont is divided from the plain along the "fall line," where early mill owners once set their waterwheels to take advantage of the descending streams. Many towns—such as both state capitals, Raleigh, North Carolina, and Columbia, South Carolina—grew up naturally along this fall line. West of the Piedmont lies the Appalachian mountain chain. North Carolina holds the chain's highest peaks, including the tallest, Mount Mitchell.

SC ★ The Palmetto State

The Carolinas were among the thirteen original colonies. In fact, the first English settlement in the Americas was founded on Roanoke Island off North Carolina in 1585—although it mysteriously disappeared soon after. By the early 1800's, cotton and tobacco plantations supported by slaves had become a way of life. The first shots of the Civil War were fired at Fort Sumter, South Carolina, and after the war, a long period of poverty followed. In the years following the war, many textile mills employed people, as they do today, although low wages and competition from abroad have been problems.

North Carolina's Outer Banks

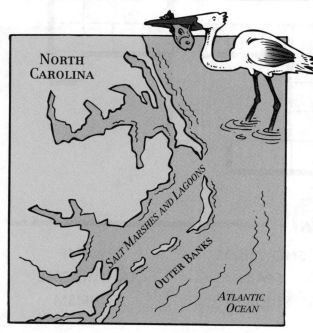

Today, most Carolina residents work in tourism and manufacturing. Tobacco is the biggest crop, and cigarette making is a large industry, especially around Raleigh in North Carolina. Since the 1970's, the population of each state has been growing, partly because of new electronics industries and university growth. In North Carolina, a "research triangle" has grown up around the University of North Carolina at Chapel Hill, Duke University, and North Carolina State. And visitors come to the Carolinas not only for the beaches but also to see historic sites such as the colonial era gardens and homes in Charleston, South Carolina.

Read the sentences about North Carolina and South Carolina.
Then complete the sentences by filling in each blank.
Use the word list if you need help.

★ The South Carolina city of _____ is famous for its colonial era gardens and houses.

★ The first mills along the fall line depended on _____ for power.

★ The University of North Carolina at Chapel Hill, Duke University, and North Carolina

State form the North Carolina _____ triangle.

★ The islands off North Carolina are called the _____ Banks.

★ _____ is the major crop in both Carolinas.

★ The first shots of the Civil War were fired at Fort _____.

★ The _____ line lies between the coastal plain and the Piedmont.

★ Mount _____ is the tallest Appalachian mountain.

★ Salty _____ help separate the Outer Banks from the North Carolina mainland.

★ North Carolina was the site of the _____ English settlement in America.

Word List

Charleston	first	Outer	Tobacco
fall	marshes	research	water
	Mitchell	Sumter	

Virginia and Maryland

Virginia and Maryland have a geography similar to the rest of the states that line the Atlantic Ocean in the South. Flat coastal plains, sometimes called the tidewater region, give way to the slightly higher, rolling Piedmont. On the western edge of each state is part of the Appalachian range named the Blue Ridge. In Virginia, it is called the ridge and valley region. Maryland has a special physical feature, the Chesapeake Bay. The part of Maryland east of the bay is known as the Eastern Shore. Only the southeastern tip of Maryland extends out to the Atlantic, where Ocean City welcomes beachgoers. Between Virginia and Maryland flows the Potomac, on which Washington, D.C., is located. The national capital strongly affects both sides.

The capital of Maryland, Annapolis, is a small city on the western shore of the Chesapeake. Baltimore, to the north on the same side, is by far Maryland's biggest city. The area between Baltimore and Washington, D.C., is so urbanized that it is really one huge metropolitan area. In the past, Baltimore was host to heavy industries, but today, many people work for government agencies or in computer software or biotech industries.

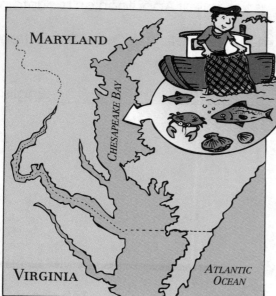

Fishermen work the waters of Chesapeake Bay, gathering crabs, clams, oysters, and many kinds of fish, but water pollution is endangering the catch.

Virginia is a much larger state, but it, too, is home to many government institutions and businesses that serve the national government. You can still visit many places to remember Virginia's rich history, such as Jamestown, site of the first lasting English colony, and colonial Williamsburg. The capital of the state, Richmond, was once the capital of the Confederacy. Civil War battlefields all over the state show how hard the war was fought there.

A good place to see natural Virginia is in Shenandoah National Park, where hardwood forests blanket the Blue Ridge. They turn lovely colors in the fall.

Use the word list to help you find the words about Virginia
and Maryland that are hidden in the block below.
Some of the words are hidden backward or diagonally.

```
C P C H E S A P E A K E B A Y V
E T P W S K I J A M E S T O W N
A T C I P E F T A Z J U H G Y D
R N D F D T S O U T H C R D C B
J E N M E A Y M V I E U I E A A
Y M O P G N I A O T B P C O R T
G N T O D N S C O S H J H E E T
T R G T I A S I M X O C M K D L
I E N O R P B A L T I M O R E E
D V I M E O I O D A J X N B F F
E O H A U L O S P R G Q D P N I
W G S C L I T D N J M C U Q O E
A M A I B S E A T L A N T I C L
T T W W H R O C E A N C I T Y D
E U N B L D H A O D N A N E H S
R E A S T E R N S H O R E W C A
```

Word List

ANNAPOLIS
ATLANTIC
BALTIMORE
BATTLEFIELDS
BIOTECH

BLUE RIDGE
CHESAPEAKE BAY
CONFEDERACY
EASTERN SHORE
GOVERNMENT

JAMESTOWN
OCEAN CITY
PIEDMONT
POTOMAC
RICHMOND

SHENANDOAH
SOUTH
TIDEWATER
WASHINGTON DC
WILLIAMSBURG

Washington, District of Columbia

Washington, D.C., is the capital of the United States. The city of Washington is not a state. It is in a special district called the District of Columbia. This area of land, located between Virginia and Maryland on the bank of the Potomac River, is controlled by Congress. As the capital, Washington, D.C., is a symbol of unity for all the states. It is the center for the nation's government. Today, the District totals about sixty-eight square miles. The Washington metropolitan area is one of the largest urban areas in the nation; it includes suburbs in Virginia as well as those in Maryland extending up to Baltimore.

Washington, D.C., was planned by Congress to be the nation's capital, and Congress decided to name the city after the nation's first president. George Washington never lived there, but he appointed a French architect, Pierre L'Enfant, to design the city. In 1800, the government moved to Washington, and John Adams became the first president to live in the White House. The Capitol, intended to be the meeting place of Congress, was barely finished when the British burned it during the War of 1812. It was promptly rebuilt. Today, most Washingtonians make a living by working in government, providing services, or working in tourism. Young and old alike enjoy the Smithsonian Institution museums and other attractions located along the Mall. Visitors come to Washington all year, but a favorite time is in spring when the famous cherry trees, a gift from Japan, are in bloom around town.

Washington, D.C., was at first entirely controlled by Congress. Citizens now elect their own city council and mayor, but Congress still has the right to regulate the city and its spending. The people of Washington, D.C., elect a representative to Congress, but that person cannot vote on laws. Even though the city is so important to the nation, poverty and crime have been serious problems there.

**Read the clues about Washington, D.C.
Then complete the puzzle using the word list on the next page.**

★ Across ★

1. City where government is, such as Washington, D.C.
5. The Washington _____ is at the far end of the Mall from the Capitol.
6. People who burned the Capitol on the War of 1812
8. Name of the institution that has many museums in Washington, D.C.
9. Kind of pink blossoms famous in Washington, D.C.
10. Name of the river that borders Washington, D.C.
11. Washington, D.C.'s, only one has no vote in Congress.
12. Name of the grassy rectangle extending from the capitol

Down

2. Last name of the first president to live in the White House
3. Washington, D.C., is not in a state but in a _____.
4. Most people in Washington, D.C., work in services, tourism, or _____.
7. Group finally responsible for city government in Washington, D.C.
9. Building where Congress meets

Washington, D.C.

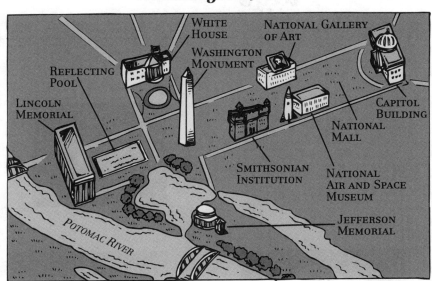

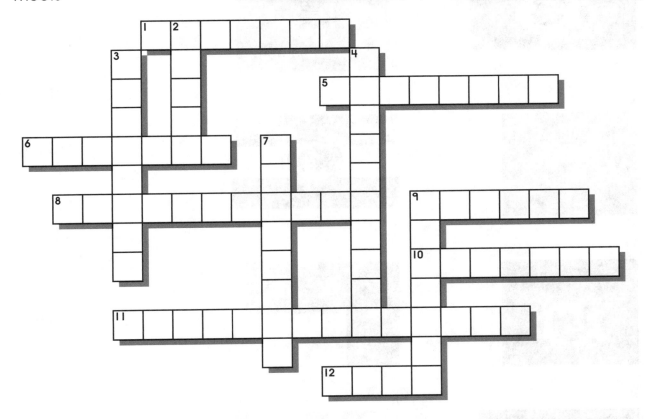

Word List

ADAMS	CHERRY	GOVERNMENT	POTOMAC
BRITISH	CONGRESS	MALL	REPRESENTATIVE
CAPITAL	DISTRICT	MONUMENT	SMITHSONIAN
CAPITOL			

State Flags

Do you know your state flags? Match each flag to its state.

a.

b.

c.

d.

e.

f.

g.

h.

i.

j.

_____ Louisiana

_____ Oklahoma

_____ New York

_____ Virginia

_____ Missouri

_____ North Carolina

_____ New Mexico

_____ Maine

_____ Minnesota

_____ New Hampshire

State Flags

Do you know your state flags? Match each flag to its state.

a.

f.

b.

g.

c.

h.

d.

i.

e.

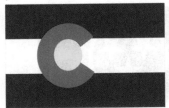

j.

_____ Vermont

_____ Colorado

_____ Kentucky

_____ Wisconsin

_____ Mississippi

_____ West Virginia

_____ Utah

_____ Wyoming

_____ Iowa

_____ Idaho

State Flags

Do you know your state flags? Match each flag to its state.

a.

b.

c.

d.

e.

f.

g.

h.

i.

j.

_____ Michigan

_____ California

_____ Rhode Island

_____ Tennessee

_____ Washington

_____ Montana

_____ Arizona

_____ South Dakota

_____ Indiana

_____ Hawaii

State Flags

Do you know your state flags? Match each flag to its state.

a.

b.

c.

d.

e.

f.

g.

h.

i.

j.

_____ Arkansas

_____ Florida

_____ Illinois

_____ Pennsylvania

_____ Ohio

_____ Nevada

_____ South Carolina

_____ Georgia

_____ North Dakota

_____ Kansas

State Flags

Do you know your state flags? Match each flag to its state.

a.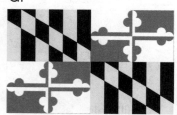

f.

b.

g.

c.

h.

d.

i.

e.

j.

_____ Connecticut

_____ Alaska

_____ Maryland

_____ Oregon

_____ New Jersey

_____ Alabama

_____ Massachusetts

_____ Delaware

_____ Nebraska

_____ Texas

Abbreviate the States

When you mail a letter or postcard to someone, the state in the address is always abbreviated using two capital letters. See how many postal abbreviations you know by filling in the correct abbreviation next to each state on pages 310 and 311.

_____ Alabama   _____ Delaware   _____ Indiana   _____ Maryland

_____ Alaska   _____ Florida   _____ Iowa   _____ Massachusetts

_____ Arizona   _____ Georgia   _____ Kansas   _____ Michigan

_____ Arkansas   _____ Hawaii   _____ Kentucky   _____ Minnesota

_____ California   _____ Idaho   _____ Louisiana   _____ Mississippi

_____ Colorado   _____ Illinois   _____ Maine   _____ Missouri

_____ Connecticut

John Q. Smith
123 Broad St.
Somewhere, OH 00000

USA
34

Jane Doe
123 Main Street
Anytown, OH 00000

Abbreviate the States

_____ Montana   _____ North Carolina   _____ Rhode Island   _____ Vermont

_____ Nebraska   _____ North Dakota   _____ South Carolina   _____ Virginia

_____ Nevada   _____ Ohio   _____ South Dakota   _____ Washington

_____ New Hampshire _____ Oklahoma   _____ Tennessee   _____ West Virginia

_____ New Jersey   _____ Oregon   _____ Texas   _____ Wisconsin

_____ New Mexico   _____ Pennsylvania   _____ Utah   _____ Wyoming

_____ New York

Dear Jane,

USA 20

Jane Doe
123 Main Street
Anytown, OH 00000

State Riddles

Read the riddles below about the U.S. states. You may know some of the answers right away—other riddles may be more difficult, so you will have to do some research. Then, solve each riddle by filling in the name of the state that is being described.

I am the biggest state. The highest peak in the U.S., Mt. McKinley, is located in me.

Which state am I?_____

I can "show" you a lot. Jefferson City is my capital. In the summer of 1993, much of

my land flooded. Which state am I?_____

Abraham Lincoln was born in me. A famous derby is held in me. The nation's gold

vault is in my Fort Knox. Which state am I?_____

La Salle claimed my area for France in 1682. The U.S. bought me from France in 1803.

I am the 18th state. Which state am I?_____

I am often called the Great Lakes State because I touch four of the five. My Battle

Creek is the largest producer of breakfast cereal. Which state am I?

_____

My Jamestown was the site of the first permanent English settlement in America.

Patrick Henry gave his famous speech in my Appomattox Court House. Which state

am I? _____

Montgomery is my capital. My state flower is the camellia. Which state am I?

_____

I contain the Grand Canyon. Phoenix is my capital. Without irrigation, half of me

would be desert. Which state am I?_____

I was the home of seven U.S. presidents. The Pro Football Hall of Fame is located in my

Canton. Which state am I?_____

State Riddles

Here are more riddles about the U.S. states. You may know some of the answers right away—other riddles may be more difficult, so you will have to do some research. Then, solve each riddle by filling in the name of the state that is being described.

I am big—220 times the size of Rhode Island! I have the most farms, farmland, cattle, horses, and sheep in the nation. Which state am I?_____

I am the "Land of Opportunity." Bill Clinton was born in me. Little Rock is my capital. Which state am I?_____

My people are "Hoosiers." I am the 19th state. The University of Notre Dame is located in me. Which state am I?_____

I got my name from the Indians. Bismarck is my capital. I am the Flickertail State. Which state am I?_____

I am the 50th state. My Pearl Harbor is very famous. Diamond Head is one of my most famous extinct volcanoes. Which state am I?

_____

I was the first state to secede from the Union. My Fort Sumter was the place where the Civil War began. I am the Palmetto State. Which state am I?

_____

I am the smallest state. Roger Williams founded me in 1636. I produce the most costume jewelry in the world. Which state am I?_____

I am the First State. I was named for Lord De La Warr. I was the first state to ratify the new constitution in 1787. Which state am I?_____

I am the Gopher State. My Mesabi Range contains much iron ore. St. Paul is my capital. Which state am I?_____

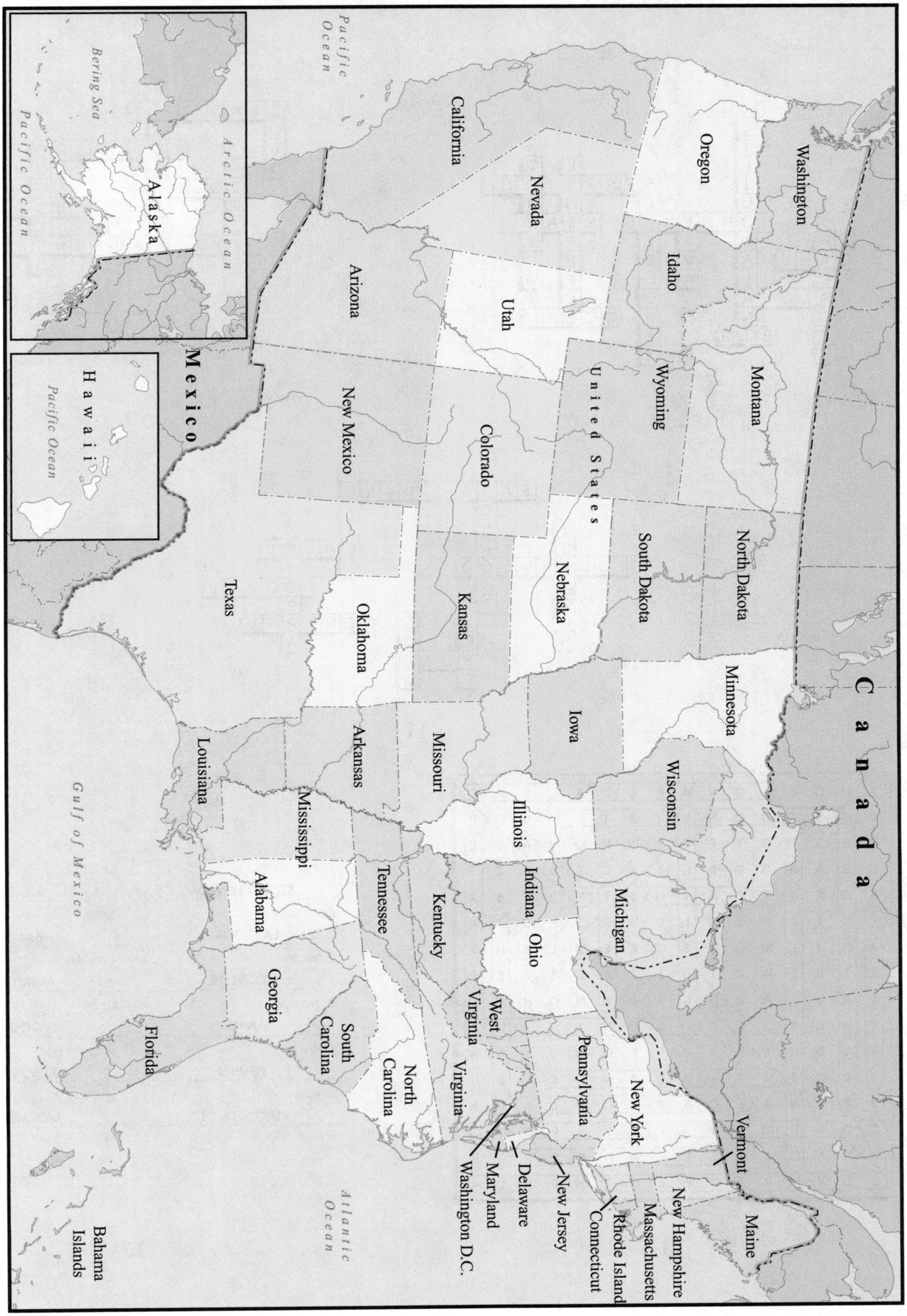

Pacific Ocean

Bering Sea

Pacific Ocean

Alaska

Arctic Ocean

Hawaii

Pacific Ocean

Mexico

Pacific Ocean

California

Oregon

Washington

Nevada

Idaho

Arizona

Utah

Montana

United States

Wyoming

New Mexico

Colorado

North Dakota

South Dakota

Nebraska

Minnesota

Canada

Texas

Oklahoma

Kansas

Iowa

Wisconsin

Louisiana

Arkansas

Missouri

Illinois

Indiana

Michigan

Gulf of Mexico

Mississippi

Alabama

Tennessee

Kentucky

Ohio

West Virginia

Pennsylvania

New York

Vermont

Georgia

South Carolina

North Carolina

Virginia

Washington D.C.

Maryland

Delaware

New Jersey

Connecticut

Rhode Island

Massachusetts

New Hampshire

Maine

Florida

Bahama Islands

Atlantic Ocean

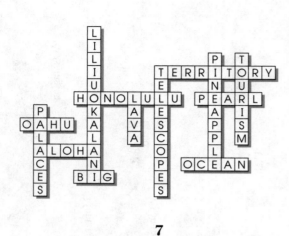

7

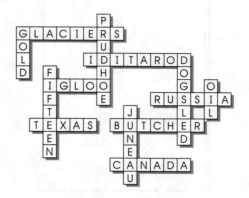

9

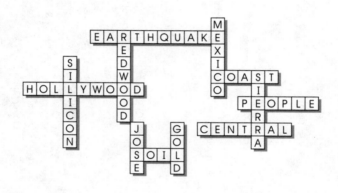

11

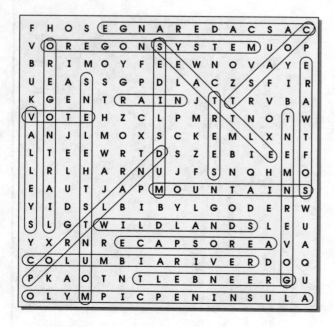

13

RARIES VANEDA	VERSIL
SIERRA NEVADA	**SILVER**
SAL GASEV	SABNI
LAS VEGAS	**BASIN**
STORUIST	NIFRGMA
TOURISTS	**FARMING**
CYNOSAN	LODG
CANYONS	**GOLD**
NOUYG	SACNOR TYIC
YOUNG	**CARSON CITY**
IGANIRVI CTYI	SONMROM
VIRGINIA CITY	**MORMONS**

15

Puzzle 17 (crossword solution)

Across/Down answers: SILVER, GLACIER, GUIDE, DIVIDE, BOISE, RESERVATION, BUFFALO, LUMBER, SNAKE, HELENA, POTATO, PERCE, COEUR, NORTHERN

★ **Wind** _____ River is a large Native American reservation in central Wyoming.

★ Wyoming is home to _____ **Shoshone** _____ and Arapaho people.

★ Esther Hobart _____ **Morris** _____ sought equality for women in Wyoming Territory.

★ America's oldest national park, located in Wyoming, is **Yellowstone** _____ .

★ The Colorado town of _____ **Aspen** _____ is famous as a ski resort.

★ The _____ **Anasazi** _____ were ancient Native American people who built cliff dwellings.

★ **Colorado** _____ has the highest average elevation in the United States.

★ Wyoming is known as the _____ **Equality** _____ State.

★ The U.S. _____ **Air** _____ Force has an academy in Colorado Springs.

★ Wyoming has fewer _____ **people** _____ than Colorado.

17

19

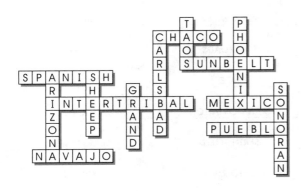

21

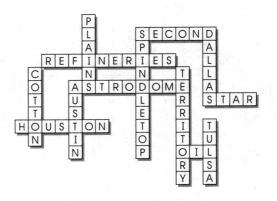

23

25

Crossword (page 25):
GOLD, HOMESTAKE, MISSOURI, CUSTER, BLACK, RUSHMORE, BISMARCK, WOUNDED, WHEAT, HARRISON, HOMESTEAD, HORSES, HEAD

27

PEAKOT	TAMARIGUUCFNN
TOPEKA	**MANUFACTURING**
LACGUERRITU	ERACLE
AGRICULTURE	**CEREAL**
CENSNIARU	ACRULINMEA
INSURANCE	**UNICAMERAL**
THICAIW	THAEW
WICHITA	**WHEAT**
SELARPNAI	SHEDMIONETAG
AIRPLANES	**HOMESTEADING**
SED NOMIES	NNOLCLI
DES MOINES	**LINCOLN**

29

Word search grid:

```
D F W Y D A I R Y F A R M S W Y
M I C H I G A N N O S I D A M P
A B T K V B C F E J S O U T I B
L A K E S Q F I I Z E N S A L L
L G L U C X T O E F M A O M W H
O L L A N S I N G P B N T H A I
F I S H I N G R E D L O P F U L
A P T R I S L E R O Y A L E K A
M R I L D K V O M D L N J V E T
E M O Z R J F Y A S I U X G E O
R H R O G L H E N T N E P C S S
I D T W I N C I T I E S A H X E
C K E C W G B A K U C R Q E S N
A W D X Q U V I H I M J V E D N
Z B W I S C O N S I N F R S C I
A N S E K A L T A E R G W E R M
```

31

SPERASCKYR	SLUBL
SKYSCRAPER	**BULLS**
DARRLOAIS	COLINNL
RAILROADS	**LINCOLN**
ZAJZ	FLARDAMN
JAZZ	**FARMLAND**
SPOTRAINTOTNAR	COGHACI
TRANSPORTATION	**CHICAGO**
IRDSNEGPFIL	RSEAS REWTO
SPRINGFIELD	**SEARS TOWER**
OHO RIERV	INARG
OHIO RIVER	**GRAIN**

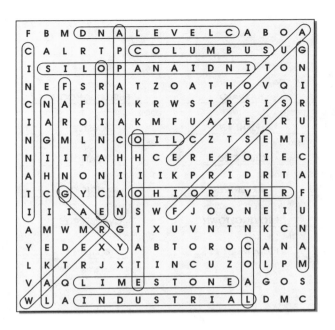

33

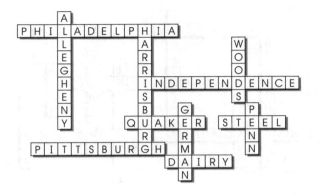

35

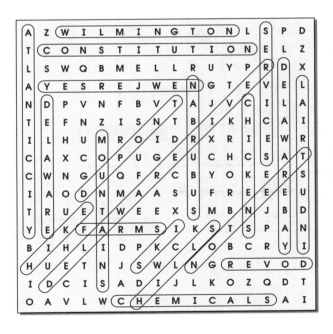

37

39

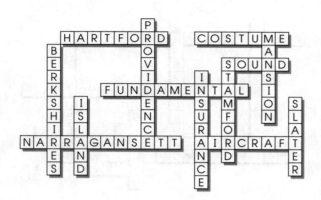

41

43

STERFOS
FORESTS

TIOUMRS
TOURISM

REBALLI
LIBERAL

CROONCD
CONCORD

RISESK
SKIERS

BLUPERIC
REPUBLIC

RULMEB
LUMBER

IMAPACHLN
CHAMPLAIN

SMNOIUANT
MOUNTAINS

PEOERRTF
FREEPORT

TELNIECO
ELECTION

TRAEING
GRANITE

45

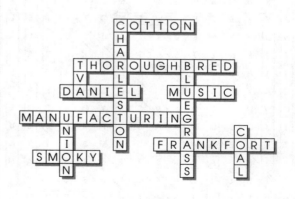

47

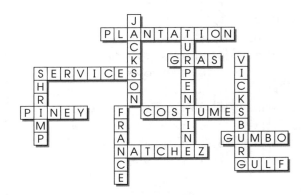

49

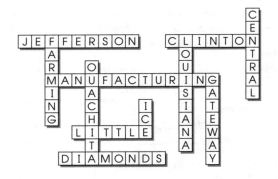

51

TALANTA	**ATLANTA**
SEFORT	**FOREST**
ELEST	**STEEL**
CASPAHALAPIN	**APPALACHIANS**
GONERTYMOM	**MONTGOMERY**
FILEDILW	**WILDLIFE**
TAPNLOAINT	**PLANTATION**
AFEEDORNCCY	**CONFEDERACY**
GAMRIMINBH	**BIRMINGHAM**
DOEMIPNT	**PIEDMONT**
VICLI SHRIGT	**CIVIL RIGHTS**
TOCNOT	**COTTON**

53

55

★ The South Carolina city of _____ **Charleston** _____ is famous for its colonial era gardens and houses

★ The first mills along the fall line depended on _____ **water** _____ for power.

★ The University of North Carolina at Chapel Hill, Duke University, and North Carolina State form the North Carolina _____ **research** _____ triangle.

★ The islands off North Carolina are called the _____ **Outer** _____ Banks.

★ **Tobacco** _____ is the major crop in both Carolinas

★ The first shots of the Civil War were fired at Fort _____ **Sumter** _____ .

★ The _____ **fall** _____ line lies between the coastal plain and the Piedmont.

★ Mount _____ **Mitchell** _____ is the tallest Appalachian mountain.

★ Salty _____ **marshes** _____ help separate the Outer Banks from the North Carolina mainland.

★ North Carolina was the site of the _____ **first** _____ English settlement in America.

57

```
C P C H E S A P E A K E B A Y V
E T P W S K I J A M E S T O W N
A T C I P E F T A Z J U H G Y D
R N D F D T S O U T H C R D C B
J E N M E A Y M V I E U I E A A
Y M O P G N I A O T B P C O R T
    T G N I A S C O S H J E E T
T R E O T I P S I M X O C M K D L
I E V I O R S B A L T I M O R E E
D O I M E O I O D A J X N B F F
E H A U L O S P R G Q D P N I
W G S C L I T D N J M C U Q O E
A I B S E A T L A N T I C L
T W W H R O C E A N C I T Y D
U N B L D H A O D N A N E H S
R E A S T E R N S H O R E W C A
```

59

```
        C A P I T A L
        D           G
    D   A       M O N U M E N T
    I   M       O   V
B R I T I S H   C   E
    S       C O N G R E S S
    T       O   R
S M I T H S O N I A N   C H E R R Y
    R       G   M   A
    I       R   E   P O T O M A C
    C       E   N   I
    T   R E P R E S E N T A T I V E
    S       S   T   O
            M A L L
```

61

a.
b.
c.
d.
e.
f.
g.
h.
i.
j.

j Louisiana
g Oklahoma
d New York
e Virginia
h Missouri
i North Carolina
a New Mexico
f Maine
b Minnesota
c New Hampshire

62

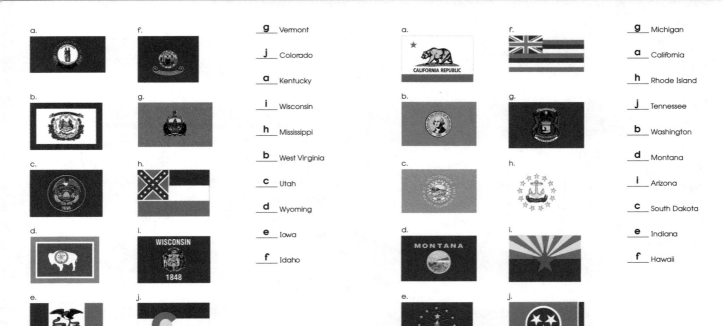

63

a.

f.

g. Vermont

j. Colorado

a. Kentucky

i. Wisconsin

h. Mississippi

b. West Virginia

c. Utah

d. Wyoming

e. Iowa

f. Idaho

64

g. Michigan

a. California

h. Rhode Island

j. Tennessee

b. Washington

d. Montana

i. Arizona

c. South Dakota

e. Indiana

f. Hawaii

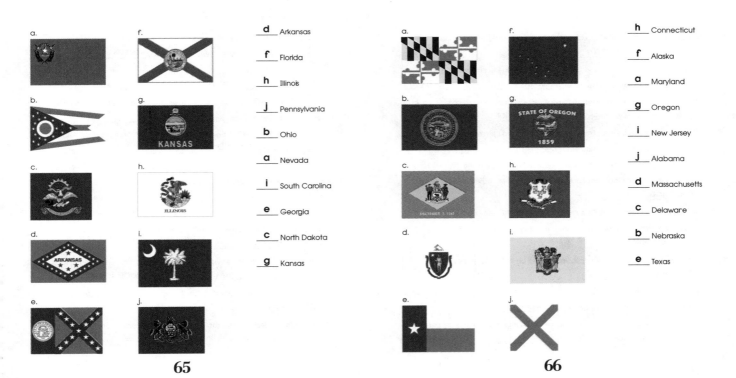

65

d. Arkansas

f. Florida

h. Illinois

j. Pennsylvania

b. Ohio

a. Nevada

i. South Carolina

e. Georgia

c. North Dakota

g. Kansas

66

h. Connecticut

f. Alaska

a. Maryland

g. Oregon

i. New Jersey

j. Alabama

d. Massachusetts

c. Delaware

b. Nebraska

e. Texas

AL	Alabama	DE	Delaware	IN	Indiana	MD	Maryland
AK	Alaska	FL	Florida	IA	Iowa	MA	Massachusetts
AZ	Arizona	GA	Georgia	KS	Kansas	MI	Michigan
AR	Arkansas	HI	Hawaii	KY	Kentucky	MN	Minnesota
CA	California	ID	Idaho	LA	Louisiana	MS	Mississippi
CO	Colorado	IL	Illinois	ME	Maine	MO	Missouri
CT	Connecticut						

MT	Montana	NC	North Carolina	RI	Rhode Island	VT	Vermont
NE	Nebraska	ND	North Dakota	SC	South Carolina	VA	Virginia
NV	Nevada	OH	Ohio	SD	South Dakota	WA	Washington
NH	New Hampshire	OK	Oklahoma	TN	Tennessee	WV	West Virginia
NJ	New Jersey	OR	Oregon	TX	Texas	WI	Wisconsin
NM	New Mexico	PA	Pennsylvania	UT	Utah	WY	Wyoming
NY	New York						

67

68

I am the biggest state. The highest peak in the U.S., Mt. McKinley, is located in me. Which state am I? **Alaska**

I can "show" you a lot. Jefferson City is my capital. In the summer of 1993, much of my land flooded. Which state am I? **Missouri**

Abraham Lincoln was born in me. A famous derby is held in me. The nation's gold vault is in my Fort Knox. Which state am I? **Kentucky**

La Salle claimed my area for France in 1682. The U.S. bought me from France in 1803. I am the 18th state. Which state am I? **Louisiana**

I am often called the Great Lakes State because I touch four of the five. My Battle Creek is the largest producer of breakfast cereal. Which state am I?
Michigan

My Jamestown was the site of the first permanent English settlement in America. Patrick Henry gave his famous speech in my Appomattox Court House. Which state am I? **Virginia**

Montgomery is my capital. My state flower is the camellia. Which state am I?
Alabama

I contain the Grand Canyon. Phoenix is my capital. Without irrigation, half of me would be desert. Which state am I? **Arizona**

I was the home of seven U.S. presidents. The Pro Football Hall of Fame is located in my Canton. Which state am I? **Ohio**

69

I am big—220 times the size of Rhode Island! I have the most farms, farmland, cattle horses, and sheep in the nation. Which state am I? **Texas**

I am the "Land of Opportunity." Bill Clinton was born in me. Little Rock is my capital. Which state am I? **Arkansas**

My people are "Hoosiers." I am the 19th state. The University of Notre Dame is located in me. Which state am I? **Indiana**

I got my name from the Indians. Bismarck is my capital. I am the Flickertail State. Which state am I? **North Dakota**

I am the 50th state. My Pearl Harbor is very famous. Diamond Head is one of my most famous extinct volcanoes. Which state am I?
Hawaii

I was the first state to secede from the Union. My Fort Sumter was the place where the Civil War began. I am the Palmetto State. Which state am I?
South Carolina

I am the smallest state. Roger Williams founded me in 1636. I produce the most costume jewelry in the world. Which state am I? **Rhode Island**

I am the First State. I was named for Lord De La Warr. I was the first state to ratify the new constitution in 1787. Which state am I? **Delaware**

I am the Gopher State. My Mesabi Range contains much iron ore. St. Paul is my capital. Which state am I? **Minnesota**

70